Confronting the "Enemy Within"

Security Intelligence, the Police, and Counterterrorism in Four Democracies

PETER CHALK, WILLIAM ROSENAU

This research in the public interest was supported by RAND, using discretionary funds made possible by the generosity of RAND's donors, the fees earned on client-funded research, and independent research and development (IR&D) funds provided by the Department of Defense.

Library of Congress Cataloging-in-Publication Data

Chalk, Peter.
    Confronting the "enemy within" : security intelligence, the police, and counterterrorism in four democracies / Peter Chalk, William Roseanau.
      p. cm.
    "MG-100."
    Includes bibliographical references.
    ISBN 0-8330-3513-4 (pbk. : alk. paper)
    1. Terrorism—Prevention—Cross-cultural studies. 2. Intelligence service—Cross-cultural studies. 3. Internal security—Cross-cultural studies. 4. Great Britain. MI5. 5. France. Direction de la surveillance du territoire. 6. Canadian Security Intelligence Service. 7. Australian Security Intelligence Organization. I. Rosenau, William. II. Rand Corporation. III.Title.

HV6431 .C443 2004
363.32—dc22
                                   2003024359

The RAND Corporation is a nonprofit research organization providing objective analysis and effective solutions that address the challenges facing the public and private sectors around the world. RAND's publications do not necessarily reflect the opinions of its research clients and sponsors.

RAND® is a registered trademark.

Cover design by Stephen Bloodsworth

Published 2004 by the RAND Corporation
1700 Main Street, P.O. Box 2138, Santa Monica, CA 90407-2138
1200 South Hayes Street, Arlington, VA 22202-5050
201 North Craig Street, Suite 202, Pittsburgh, PA 15213-1516
RAND URL: http://www.rand.org/
To order RAND documents or to obtain additional information, contact
Distribution Services: Telephone: (310) 451-7002;
Fax: (310) 451-6915; Email: order@rand.org

Preface

This report considers the origin, development, and functions of selected non-U.S. intelligence organizations, assessing their role in terrorism threat mitigation, their relationship with law enforcement agencies, and the means and modalities by which they are controlled and monitored. The analysis is intended to help inform debate within the United States on the advisability of creating a dedicated information collection and surveillance body that operates outside the existing structure of the Federal Bureau of Investigation (FBI).

The research presented here is derived exclusively from open sources: published books, newspaper and other secondary sources, public government documents, and interviews with academics and active and retired law enforcement and intelligence officials. The study was supported through the provision of independent research and development funds provided by RAND Public Safety and Justice (PSJ), a division of the RAND Corporation.

Jack Riley, Director of PSJ, provided overall supervision for this research. Comments on the study are welcomed and should be directed to the authors (Peter Chalk or William Rosenau) or to Dr. Riley.

The RAND Corporation Quality Assurance Process

Peer review is an integral part of all RAND research projects. Prior to publication, this document, as with all documents in the RAND monograph series, was subject to a quality assurance process to ensure that the research meets several standards, including the following: The problem is well formulated; the research approach is well designed and well executed; the data and assumptions are sound; the findings are useful and advance knowledge; the implications and recommendations follow logically from the findings and are explained thoroughly; the documentation is accurate, understandable, cogent, and temperate in tone; the research demonstrates understanding of related previous studies; and the research is relevant, objective, independent, and balanced. Peer review is conducted by research professionals who were not members of the project team.

RAND routinely reviews and refines its quality assurance process and also conducts periodic external and internal reviews of the quality of its body of work. For additional details regarding the RAND quality assurance process, visit http://www.rand.org/standards/.

Contents

Table

Summary

In the aftermath of the September 11, 2001 terrorist attacks, the U.S. Federal Bureau of Investigation (FBI) was widely criticized for failing to prevent the strikes on the World Trade Center and the Pentagon. Critics charged that the bureau, while superbly qualified to investigate terrorist incidents *after* the fact, was grossly ill equipped to *prevent* attacks, given its strong law enforcement and prosecutorial culture. Deliberation has subsequently centered on the advisability of creating a new domestic intelligence service outside the existing structure of the FBI. Proponents argue that establishing an agency that is solely concerned with information gathering, analysis, assessment, and dissemination would decisively ameliorate the type of hybrid reactive-proactive mission that so often confounds police-based intelligence units. Opponents counter that an institution of this sort would merely undermine civil liberties, unduly hinder interagency communication and coordination, and create additional barriers between intelligence and law enforcement.

Understanding the experience of domestic intelligence bureaus in the United Kingdom, France, Canada, and Australia—all of which are close U.S. allies based on similar democratic values—can help inform this debate. While the agencies in each of these countries have inevitably been shaped by the particular political and security environment in which each has had to operate, it is possible to extrapolate positive and negative themes that are common across the four services concerned. These lessons highlight practical and operational considerations that would be extremely valuable in guiding counterterrorist initiatives that might take place in the United States.

Domestic Intelligence in the United Kingdom, France, Canada, and Australia

The United Kingdom, France, Canada, and Australia all retain dedicated structures to collect, assess, and disseminate information on domestic terrorist challenges within their respective territorial jurisdictions. These include the UK Security Service (also known as MI5),[1] France's Direction de la Surveillance du Territoire (Directorate of Territorial Security, or DST), the Canadian Security Intelligence Service (CSIS), and the Australian Security Intelligence Organisation (ASIO). In each of these cases, the agency in question has no powers of arrest, is separated from wider law enforcement but retains a close working relationship with the police, is primarily concerned with proactive threat mitigation, and is governed by specific accountability and oversight provisions.

Several features of these models are worthy of note.

Strengths
On the positive side, at least eight observations stand out:

First, all four countries vest domestic counterterrorism intelligence in the hands of agencies that have no functional law enforcement powers of arrest or detention. This has ensured the emergence of bureaus that are able to devote all their resources to preemptive information gathering.

Second, the United Kingdom, France, Canada, and Australia make extensive use of their intelligence services in local community information gathering. These activities have availed a useful "force multiplier" effect that has greatly enhanced the potential scope of national surveillance efforts. In addition, they have helped to give the

---

[1]"Security Services" and "MI5" are used interchangeably throughout this report.

intelligence services more of a "public face" and at least provided a means to explain the nature, rationale, and purpose of their work.

Third, a primary emphasis on the active recruitment and sourcing of terrorist insiders has consistently underscored the work of MI5, the DST, CSIS, and ASIO. Framing overall data collection efforts in a human-based context of this sort has been highly effective in disrupting operational cells and providing real-time intelligence on extremist intentions, capabilities, resources, and evolving dynamics. Just as importantly, it has contributed to well-developed physical protection programs, which has allowed for greater flexibility in target hardening and has helped to mitigate the wasteful and inefficient allocation of resources.

Fourth, the institution of comprehensive checks and balances has formed an integral component of the intelligence infrastructure in the Canadian, Australian, and, to a somewhat lesser extent, British cases. This has not only provided a transparent medium through which to demonstrate the utility of the intelligence function in counterterrorism (to both politicians and the general public), but it has also helped to lend a degree of confidence that only balanced and controlled responses will be instituted in the name of national security.

Fifth, the security intelligence agencies in each of these countries stresses the importance of developing regular terrorist threat assessments that police forces as well industry can use to design viable and sustainable counterstrategies. These analyses have played a highly instrumental role in national counterterrorist planning, which has, in turn, fed prudent decisionmaking about how best to allocate resources for future threat mitigation.

Sixth, the United Kingdom, France, Canada, and Australia have all been able to draw on a wider, more diverse intelligence recruitment pool by stint of having internal security services that are not bounded or defined by the strictures of a domestic policing environment. The availability of personnel who would not normally be drawn to a law enforcement profession has helped foster rounded, creative, and forward-looking analytical assessments that have straddled both the tactical and strategic dimensions of the so-called tasking, processing, exploitation, and dissemination chain.

Seventh, the existence of dedicated domestic security services in the United Kingdom, France, and Australia has worked to "smooth" information coordination with the foreign spy services in each country. This has been of enormous practical importance in the modern era of "globalized terror," in which extremist threats to the national interest no longer accord to a neat internal-external dichotomy.

Finally, divesting the intelligence function from law enforcement has necessarily meant that MI5, ASIO, CSIS, and the DST have had to operate in close tandem with their respective national police forces in terms of terrorist arrest, detention, and general threat mitigation. In all four cases, this has been achieved through the creation of dedicated coordinating bodies that have provided a central mechanism for disseminating information and availing interagency operations.

Weaknesses
It would be wrong, however, to suggest that the British, French, Canadian, and Australian models have not been without their problems. Difficulties have arisen in several areas. Operationally, the counterterrorist track record of the four agencies has been far from perfect, and there have been several instances when accepted democratic norms and operational limits have been violated in the name of counterterrorism. More pointedly, the establishment of dedicated domestic intelligence agencies vested with unique powers of covert surveillance has helped to "bureaucratically normalize" state security infrastructures that have considerable authority over the individual.

Difficulties have also been evident in terms of information dissemination. Both MI5 and CSIS have been accused of failing to pass on intelligence to relevant authorities that could have prevented several high-profile terrorist incidents, while ASIO has, on occasion, deliberately withheld information on the basis of its own idiosyncratic calculation of the national interest.

In common with the United States, the issue of trust has frequently been a major underlying factor in mitigating the effective dissemination of data among and between counterterrorism agencies and bureaus. In France, for example, coordination between the police and intelligence services has, at least historically, been subject to chronic problems of mistrust, with agencies not only failing to collaborate but moreover occasionally working at complete cross-purposes with one another.

Beyond operational and organizational matters, some fairly significant gaps in intelligence accountability and bureaucratic control have been apparent. Critics have decried parliamentary oversight arrangements in the United Kingdom—which answer directly to the prime minister—as offering only the "barest of fig leaves" in terms of comprehensive external scrutiny, arguing further that ministers and members of Parliament existing outside the privileged ring of secrecy can never hope to know the true extent of MI5 operations. Problems have been even greater in France, where no independent system of legislative control exists. The absence of viable nonexecutive mechanisms of accountability in these two countries poses particular difficulties, not least because they have periodically translated into a carte blanche counterterrorist mandate that has transcended the operational and judicial spheres.

Relevance to the United States

To be sure, significant cultural, historical, and political differences exist between the United States on the one hand and the United Kingdom, France, Canada, and Australia on the other. These dichotomies necessarily mean that intelligence institutions cannot, and indeed should not, simply be replicated from one national context to the next—irrespective of their relative efficacy in their original setting.

This being said, the four case study countries do share important defining characteristics with America. Notably, these include (1) liberal democratic traditions, (2) a common concern with stemming threats to domestic stability through robust internal security infrastructures, and (3) acceptance of the need to balance operational effectiveness in the fight against terrorism with the concomitant requirement to respect fundamental norms integral to the effective functioning of an open society. Such traits make it useful to consider how each state has organized its respective counterterrorist capabilities, if only as a benchmark for guiding possible developments in the United States.

Acknowledgments

Several people in the United Kingdom, France, Canada, and Australia were integral to the completion of this research. At their request, these individuals' names do not appear in this report. The authors do, however, acknowledge here their invaluable help in undertaking this body of work.

The authors also thank Greg Treverton of RAND and Daniel Byman of Georgetown University for their thoughtful comments on previous drafts of the manuscript. Special thanks are additionally owed to James Thomson and Jack Riley for making this report possible.

Any errors or omissions are the sole responsibility of the authors.

Abbreviations

9/11	September 11, 2001
AFP	Australian Federal Police
ASIO	Australian Security Intelligence Organisation
ASIS	Australian Secret Intelligence Service
CHOGM	Commonwealth Heads of Government Meeting
CIA	Central Intelligence Agency (U.S.)
CILAT	Comité Interministériel de Lutte Anti-Terroriste [Interministerial Liaison Committee Against Terrorism] (French)
CSIS	Canadian Security Intelligence Service
DGSE	Direction General de la Securité Exterieure (French)
DSD	Defence Signals Directorate (Australian)
DST	Direction de la Surveillance du Territoire [Directorate of Territorial Security] (French)
EDIG	Executive Directorate of the Inspector General (Canadian)
FBI	Federal Bureau of Investigation (U.S.)

FLQ	Front de Liberation du Quebec
GAO	General Accounting Office (U.S.)
GCHQ	Government Communications Headquarters (UK)
GIA	Armed Islamic Group
HMIC	Her Majesty's Inspector of Constabulary (UK)
HUMINT	human intelligence
ICG	International Crisis Group
IGIS	Inspector-General of Intelligence and Security (Australian)
INSAC	Integrated National Security Assessment Centre (Canadian)
ISC	Intelligence and Security Committee (UK)
JI	Jemaah Islamiya
JIC	Joint Intelligence Committee (UK)
JTAC	Joint Terrorism Analysis Centre (UK)
LTTE	Liberation Tigers of Tamil Eelam
MI5	Security Service (UK)
MI6	Secret Intelligence Service (UK, also known as "SIS")
MP	Member of Parliament (UK)
MPSB	Metropolitan Police Department's Special Branch (UK)
NCIS	National Criminal Intelligence Service (UK)
NCTP	National Counter-Terrorism Plan (Canadian)
PIRA	Provisional Irish Republican Army

PJC	Parliamentary Joint Committee (Australian)
PJCA	Parliamentary Joint Committee on ASIO (Australian)
PKK	Kurdish Worker's Party
PSJ	Public Safety and Justice (unit of the RAND Corporation)
RCMP	Royal Canadian Mounted Police
RIPA	Regulation of Investigatory Powers Act of 2000 (UK)
RIRA	Real Irish Republican Army
SB	Special Branch (UK)
SIRC	Security and Intelligence Review Committee (Canadian)
SIS	Secret Intelligence Service (UK, also known as "MI6")
SO13	Anti-Terrorist Branch (UK)
UCLAT	Unité de Coordination de la Lutte Anti-Terroriste [Anti-Terrorism Coordination Unit] (French)

CHAPTER ONE

Introduction

In the aftermath of the September 11, 2001 terrorist attacks, the U.S. Federal Bureau of Investigation (FBI) was widely criticized for failing to prevent the strikes on the World Trade Center and the Pentagon. More broadly, the bureau, the nation's primary agency for conducting counterterrorist intelligence operations within the United States, was faulted for failing to understand the nature, scope, and virulence of the threat posed by Osama bin Laden's terror network. Critics charged that the FBI, while superbly qualified to *investigate* terrorist incidents after the fact, was grossly ill equipped to *prevent* attacks, given its strong law enforcement and prosecutorial culture. According to Senator Richard Shelby (R-Ala.), a former chairman of the Senate Select Committee on Intelligence, the bureau had a "positive aversion to long-term strategic analysis of the sort routinely expected of intelligence agencies."[1]

Recently, FBI Director Robert S. Mueller III has undertaken a series of reforms intended to bolster the agency's counterterrorism capabilities. These include a major restructuring of the bureau's headquarters, the introduction of more advanced information and communication technology, and the creation of a new career track for intelligence analysts. Combating terrorism rather than fighting "ordi-

---

[1]Quoted in Stuart Taylor, "Spying on Terrorists," *GovExec.com*, January 13, 2003.

nary" crime has become the FBI's paramount mission, according to Mueller.[2]

However, these measures have not silenced calls for a more dramatic restructuring of the country's counterterrorism machinery.[3] Specifically, debate has centered on the advisability of creating a new domestic intelligence service outside the existing structure of the FBI. Proponents argue that establishing an agency that is solely concerned with information gathering, analysis, assessment, and dissemination (i.e., one that has no law enforcement role) would decisively ameliorate the type of hybrid reactive-proactive mission that so often confounds police-based intelligence units.[4] Opponents counter that such an agency would undermine civil liberties, unduly hinder interagency communication and coordination, and create additional barriers between intelligence and law enforcement.[5] While a policy consensus has yet to emerge, the question over whether the United States needs its own domestic security intelligence service has received added prominence with the release of Congress's joint inquiry into the

---

[2]Robert S. Mueller III, "Progress Report on the Reorganization and Refocus of the FBI," testimony before the U.S. House of Representatives Committee on Appropriations, Subcommittee on the Departments of Commerce, Justice, and State, the Judiciary, and Related Agencies, June 18, 2003.

[3]Ongoing changes in the U.S. domestic intelligence architecture also include the establishment of a Central Intelligence Agency (CIA)–FBI Terrorist Threat Integration Center (TTIC) and the creation of an Information Analysis and Infrastructure Protection Directorate within the Department of Homeland Security. For more on these developments, see "A Top Intelligence Post Goes to CIA Officer in Spy Case," *New York Times*, March 14, 2003, and "Lawmakers Worry New Terrorist Threat Integration Center Is Just Another Layer of Bureaucracy," *All Things Considered* (National Public Radio), July 23, 2003.

[4]See, for instance, Advisory Panel to Assess Domestic Response Capabilities for Terrorism Involving Weapons of Mass Destruction (also known as the Gilmore Commission), *Fourth Annual Report to the President and the Congress of the Advisory Panel to Assess Domestic Response Capabilities for Terrorism Involving Weapons of Mass Destruction,* December 15, 2002, pp. 41–47.

[5]Larry M. Wortzel, "Americans Do Not Need a New Domestic Spy Agency to Improve Intelligence and Homeland Security," *Heritage Foundation Executive Memorandum,* No. 848, January 10, 2003; "No to an American MI5," *Washington Post,* January 5, 2003.

events surrounding 9/11, which sharply criticized the FBI's failure to prevent the 2001 attacks.[6]

Understanding the experience of close allied countries that have developed dedicated domestic surveillance agencies can help inform this debate. Toward that end, this report considers the origin, development, and functions of selected non-U.S. intelligence organizations, assessing their role in terrorism threat mitigation, their relationship with law enforcement agencies, and the means and modalities by which they are controlled and monitored. These organizations are sometimes referred to as "security intelligence" agencies, a term that highlights their preventive function as well as the close working relationship between intelligence organizations and the police. In these countries, intelligence is collected not simply to inform policymakers but rather is viewed as a weapon that law enforcement agencies, private industry, and public officials can use to thwart imminent and latent terrorist attacks.

The remainder of this report is divided into six chapters. Chapters Two through Five explore the makeup of security intelligence structures in four allied countries—the United Kingdom, France, Canada, and Australia.[7] These case studies are neither meant to be comprehensive nor intended to serve as prescriptions for U.S. policy. Rather, they are intended to offer a broad overview that in each instance considers the following salient attributes: (1) the terrorist threat, (2) the security intelligence organization, (3) the relationship between that service and the police, and (4) parliamentary oversight and accountability. These features, which have been variously empha-

---

[6]U.S. Congress, Senate Select Committee on Intelligence and House Permanent Select Committee on Intelligence, *Joint Inquiry into Intelligence Community Activities Before and After the Terrorist Attacks of September 11, 2001*, December 2002, particularly pp. 243–246. See also Gordon Corera, "Report Points to Weaknesses in US Intelligence Machinery," *Jane's Intelligence Review*, September 2003, pp. 46–49.

[7]These countries were selected on the basis of the following criteria: their liberal democratic makeup, their common involvement in the international war on terrorism, their experience in countering terrorism through dedicated domestic intelligence infrastructures, and the accessibility of relevant primary and secondary data sources. This last consideration was important in excluding other potential case studies, such as Germany, India, and South Africa.

sized in the general context of arguments for and against the creation of a separate American domestic intelligence agency, are summarized in Table 1.1, which for purposes of comparison includes the United States.

Chapter Six draws on the qualitative analysis presented in Chapters Two through Five to derive a set of observables that might have relevance to the specific U.S. setting. Taken in their proper context, the lessons extrapolated from the four case studies provide a relevant framework of principles that can be used to inform U.S. decision-makers as they consider how best to arrange the nature and direction of the country's future counterterrorist security intelligence and police apparatus. Chapter Seven offers some conclusions, and the Appendix details a recent legislative amendment to Australia's ASIO Act.

Table 1.1
Key Components of Security Intelligence Structures in Five Countries

	Threat	Law Enforcement Structure	Intelligence Structure	Intelligence Oversight
United States	Substantial threat posed by international groups	No national police; very decentralized	Domestic intelligence and law enforcement combined into one agency	Extensive congressional oversight
United Kingdom	Substantial threat posed by international groups; residual domestic threats	No national police, but Metropolitan Police coordinates on counterterrorism	Specialized agencies focused on domestic and international threats	Routine executive control; limited parliamentary oversight
France	Substantial threat posed by international groups; residual domestic threats	National police and paramilitary forces; highly centralized	Specialized agencies focused on domestic and international threats	Routine executive control; no parliamentary oversight
Canada	Fundraising, recruiting, sanctuary for international terrorists	Federal structure, national force	Specialized agency focused on domestic threats	Routine executive and parliamentary control and oversight
Australia	Growing perception of vulnerability to international terrorism	Federal structure, national force	Specialized agencies focused on domestic and international threats	Routine executive and parliamentary oversight and control

CHAPTER TWO
Security Intelligence in the United Kingdom

The Terrorist Threat

For much of the past 100 years, Irish terrorists have posed the most significant internal security threat to the United Kingdom. During the "Troubles" (1969–1996), more than 3,600 people died in terrorism-related violence connected to the Protestant-Catholic sectarian conflict in Northern Ireland. Although splinter organizations like the Real Irish Republican Army (RIRA) continue to operate—indeed, this group carried out one of the deadliest terrorist attacks ever perpetrated in the United Kingdom in Omagh in August 1998—Irish paramilitary organizations no longer pose the gravest threat. Today, British authorities consider international extremist groups linked to al Qaeda to be the country's major terrorist challenge.[1] As has been the case with other West European countries, the United Kingdom has served as an important fund-raising and recruiting ground for Osama bin Laden's jihadist network, as well as a theater of operations for militant Islamic cells.[2] While a host of other foreign terrorist groups operate on British soil as well—including violent extremists from Sri Lanka, India, Turkey, and the

---

[1]See, for example, Cabinet Office, *The United Kingdom and the Campaign Against International Terrorism: Progress Report*, September 9, 2002, London: Her Majesty's Stationery Office, pp. 10–11, and Home Office, "Terrorism: What We Face" webpage, www.home office.gov.uk/terrorism/threat/face/index.html.

[2]"Quiet Lives Hid a Quest to Recruit for Global Jihad," *Daily Telegraph*, April 2, 2003.

Middle East—most of them use the country to fund-raise and recruit, but few, if any, appear to be planning attacks within the United Kingdom itself.

The Security Service ("MI5")

The United Kingdom has three national intelligence and security services, known collectively as the "Agencies":

- The **Secret Intelligence Service** (SIS, or "MI6"), the nation's external intelligence agency, uses human and technical sources and liaisons with foreign security services to produce secret intelligence on political, military, and economic issues. SIS is overseen by the foreign secretary.
- The **Government Communications Headquarters** (GCHQ), also under the foreign secretary's purview, intercepts and de-codes communications and other signals that are used to create signals intelligence, or SIGINT. GCHQ also advises govern-ment departments, the armed forces, and private industry on communications security.[3]
- **MI5**, the country's internal intelligence service, is responsible for gathering information on and assessing "covertly organized [domestic] threats to the nation," such as terrorism, espionage, and the proliferation of weapons of mass destruction.[4] The Security Service is under the authority of the home secretary.

Founded in 1909 in response to widespread official and popular concern about the rise of imperial German power, the Security Serv-ice spent the next eight decades rooting out spies, monitoring subver-sive challenges to parliamentary democracy, and vetting personnel for

---

[3]Cabinet Office, *National Intelligence Machinery*, London: Her Majesty's Stationery Office, n.d., pp. 6–7.

[4]Security Service, *The Security Service: MI5*, London: Her Majesty's Stationery Office, n.d., p. 6.

sensitive government jobs.[5] Counterterrorism was another MI5 responsibility, which became increasingly important during the upsurge in terrorism at home and abroad during the early 1970s.[6]

Throughout the 1970s and 1980s, the Security Service, the police, the military, and MI6 all claimed a share of the anti-PIRA campaign, with the attendant effect that their respective roles, missions, and functions frequently conflicted, overlapped, and blurred. On the British mainland, the police were responsible for all intelligence operations against Irish Republican terrorism, working through the Special Branch (SB)[7] of the Metropolitan Police Service.[8] However, a series of high-profile terrorist incidents in London in the early 1990s, including a mortar attack on Number 10 Downing Street, prompted the British government in 1992 to give the Security Service lead responsibility for all intelligence gathering related to Irish extremism.[9] With the end of the Cold War and the presumably less urgent requirement to monitor Eastern bloc spies and subversives, additional resources have been freed up for the counterterrorist mission (which was further helped, at least partially, by surveillance and target-penetration skills acquired during decades of communist spy hunting).[10]

---

[5]For an account of the origins of the Security Service, see Christopher Andrew, *Her Majesty's Secret Service: The Making of the British Intelligence Community*, New York: Penguin Books, 1987, p. 59.

[6]Mark Urban, *UK Eyes Alpha: The Inside Story of British Intelligence*, London: Faber and Faber Limited, 1996, pp. 49–50.

[7]Within the Metropolitan Police, a number of elements make up what is known as "special operations," which in addition to Special Branch (SO12) include Covert Operations (SO10), Intelligence (SO11), and the Anti-Terrorist Branch (SO13). For more on the activities of these specialist sections, see Metropolitan Police, "Specialist Operations," webpage, www.met.police.uk/so/index.htm.

[8]The Metropolitan Police is variously referred to as the Met or Scotland Yard. Both designations are used interchangeably throughout this report.

[9]Mark Hollingsworth and Nick Fielding, *Defending the Realm: MI5 and the Shayler Affair*, London: André Deutsch Limited, 1999, p. 127.

[10]Stella Rimington, *Open Secret: The Autobiography of the Former Director-General of MI5*, London: Hutchinson, 2001, p. 262.

In addition to monitoring Irish terrorists, MI5 tracks and assesses other terrorists deemed a threat to British national security. Monitoring other violent threats, such as neo-Nazis, animal-rights extremists, and doomsday cults, is an SB responsibility. Over the past few years, however, attention has increasingly shifted to transnational Islamic terrorist organizations, which, as noted above, now form the crux of the service's work.[11]

From 2001 to 2002, 57 percent of MI5 costs were allocated to counterterrorism, with the remainder going to counterespionage (14.4 percent), counterproliferation (2.8 percent), "emerging threats" (0.3 percent), protective security (11.0 percent), serious crime (11.5 percent), and "external assistance" (3.0 percent).[12] In pursuing its domestic security mandate, MI5 employs 2,000 people and emphasizes a broad range of information-gathering techniques that span the ambit of eavesdropping/wiretapping, electronic surveillance, and, especially, human intelligence, or HUMINT. As described in a Security Service pamphlet, these techniques are intended to

> gain the advantage over the targets of our investigations . . . which we can use to counter their activities. Over time, we try to obtain detailed knowledge about target organisations, their key personalities, infrastructure, plans and capabilities.[13]

MI5's analyses contribute to a stream of information that flows into the Joint Intelligence Committee (JIC), the British government's "main instrument for advising on priorities for intelligence gathering and for assessing its results."[14] Part of the Cabinet Office and composed of senior officials from the Agencies, the JIC provides ministers and other high-level officials with "regular intelligence assessments on a range of issues of immediate and long-term importance to national

[11]Security Service (n.d., p. 14); "Special Branch More Than Doubles in Size," *Statewatch*, September 2003; interview with security sources, London, January 31, 2003.

[12]Security Service (n.d., p. 11).

[13]Security Service (n.d., p. 6).

[14]Cabinet Office (n.d., p. 15).

interests,"[15] including terrorism. The service, through the Joint Terrorism Analysis Centre (JTAC) and in conjunction with SIS and GCHQ, also develops more-specific terrorist threat assessments that are distributed to "customers," such as the Ministry of Defence or UK diplomatic missions abroad.[16] This machinery works relatively smoothly, a function of the fact that intelligence officials, with the exception of those personnel at GCHQ's main facility in Cheltenham, work relatively near each other in Whitehall, are all bound by a culture of secrecy (backed up by the Official Secrets Act), and, until relatively recently, were recruited from similar educational and social backgrounds.[17]

On matters of protective security—that is, the defense of critical national infrastructure—the service reports to the Cabinet Office's Official Committee on Security, which develops and coordinates government policy.[18] In contrast to the United States, British policymakers have long viewed the protection of domestic economic assets as a key responsibility of the state. MI5 has identified roughly 400 key infrastructure targets within the United Kingdom, defined as those whose destruction would cause major damage to the country's economy.[19] Thus, the agency functions as a link between the state and key commercial and industrial enterprises, providing expert

---

[15]Cabinet Office (n.d., p. 15).

[16]ISC, *Inquiry into Intelligence, Assessments and Advice Prior to the Terrorist Bombings on Bali 12 October 2002*, Cmnd. 5724, London: Her Majesty's Stationery Office, December 2002b, p. 2. JTAC also distributes its assessments to local police through the SB structure. JTAC is a "virtual" organization, with personnel drawn from MI5, MI6, the police, and other agencies. Although not technically part of MI5, it reports to the Director General of the Security Service.

[17]Joanna Ensum, "Domestic Security in the United Kingdom: An Overview," in Markle Foundation Task Force, *Protecting America's Freedom in the Information Age*, New York: Markle Foundation, October 2002, p. 102.

[18]Cabinet Office, *Cabinet Office Departmental Report 2003*, Cmnd. 5926, London: Her Majesty's Stationery Office, May 2003, p. 7.

[19]Interview with security source, London, January 31, 2003. "Critical national infrastructure" includes financial services, water and sewerage, telecommunications, and energy (ISC, *Annual Report 2002–2003*, Cmnd. 5837, London: Her Majesty's Stationery Office, 2003, p. 7).

advice and training to corporate security officers and others responsible for defending critical infrastructure.[20]

In addition to the above areas, the Security Service assists British law enforcement agencies as part of a national strategy to defeat serious crime. In these cases, MI5 mostly works through the National Criminal Intelligence Service (NCIS), which serves as the main interface between the intelligence community and police criminal investigation departments.[21] Over the past decade, the Security Service has become much more involved in this aspect of the criminal justice system, most publicly by providing evidence at trials involving terrorist and serious criminal offenses.[22]

MI5 and the Police

Although MI5 is mandated to conduct surveillance operations, it has no independent arrest powers of its own. The service is thus obliged to work closely with the United Kingdom's local police forces—and in particular with each of their SBs, which serve as a "vital link between the high-level demands of national security and the local knowledge and access afforded through [local law enforcement]."[23] Indeed, SBs have been described as an "executive partner" of the Security Service that provides a "major extension [to MI5] in terms of intelligence collection capability."[24] Like the Security Service, SBs have counterespionage, counterproliferation, and countersubversive functions, although, again in common with MI5, counterterrorism is their most important mission.[25] Even though every SB has a critical

[20]Security Service (n.d., p. 9); interview with security source, London, January 31, 2003.

[21]ISC, *Annual Report 2001–2002*, Cmnd. 5542, London: Her Majesty's Stationery Office, June 2002a, p. 26.

[22]Security Service (n.d., p. 24).

[23]HMIC, *A Need to Know: HMIC Thematic Inspection of Special Branch and Ports Policing*, London: Home Office Communication Directorate, January 2003, p. 36.

[24]ISC (2003, p. 21).

[25]Home Office and Scottish Office Home and Health Department, *Guidelines on Special Branch Work in Great Britain*, London, July 1994, pp. 1–2. "Subversion" is defined as

role to play in terrorist threat mitigation (see below), it is the Metropolitan Police Department's Special Branch (MPSB) that forms the primary point of contact with MI5. Founded as the Special Irish Branch in 1883 in response to "Fenian" extremism, MPSB has over the years developed a wealth of expertise in counterterrorism operations and now represents the fundamental "oil" between the police and intelligence communities, especially in regard to the dissemination of classified information to the "cop on the beat."[26]

The SB structure is the primary instrument through which intelligence is translated into operational activity and prosecutions.[27] In their most important national role, MPSB and the 43 provincial SBs in England and Wales provide national "operational support to the Security Service for which local knowledge and access are vital." This street-level affinity ensures that each SB forms an integral component in the general process of identifying and targeting covert human intelligence sources, who are then managed by an SB unilaterally or together with MI5. Local SBs also translate assessments produced by the Security Service into more-focused analyses that can then be used to facilitate directed investigations at the provincial or municipal level.[28]

MI5 Oversight and Accountability

For much of its existence, the Security Service received little outside scrutiny, and, during the 1980s, the agency mounted vigorous coun-

---

"actions intended to overthrow or undermine parliamentary democracy by political, industrial, or violent means."

[26]Interview with Scotland Yard official, London, June 3, 2003. For more on the history of MPSB, see Andrew (1987, pp. 17–19).

[27]Interview with Metropolitan Police officer, London, January 30, 2003. All Special Branch officers are positively vetted. Outside London, this entails a rigorous process of "developed vetting" for Special Branch chiefs and their deputies, with subordinates generally processed through a more streamlined procedure that establishes them as "security checked." Within MPSB, however, the majority of personnel are subjected to a full developed vetting, thus giving them the same level of clearance as their Security Service colleagues. According to one MPS official, "This is very important as it eliminates 'you're not cleared' rows . . . a huge advantage" (email correspondence with authors, December 23, 2003).

[28]HMIC (2003, p. 56); "Special Branch More Than Doubles in Size" (2003).

tersubversion operations against what Prime Minister Margaret Thatcher famously termed the "enemy within." Targets included Arthur Scargill, the left-wing leader of the national coal miners union who was alleged to have received financial assistance from Libya, and heavily politicized pressure groups, such as the Campaign for Nuclear Disarmament and the National Council for Civil Liberties.[29] Such operations against legal and generally harmless left-wing activities badly damaged the service's reputation. As one British politician observed in 1988, "since the war, MI5 has been one of the worst and most ridiculed security services in the western alliance."[30] Widespread public criticism, together with civil actions brought before the European Court of Human Rights (ECHR), ultimately led to a number of significant reforms. Notable in this regard were the following:

- the Security Service Act of 1989, which codified MI5's rules, missions, and functions and placed the service under the home secretary's authority
- the Regulation of Investigatory Powers Act (RIPA) of 2000 and the Intelligence Services Act (ISA) of 1994, which brought procedures for intercepting communications and eavesdropping in line with the European Convention on Human Rights[31]
- the institution of an Intelligence and Security Committee (ISC) to scrutinize the "expenditure administration and policy of the United Kingdom's three intelligence and security agencies."[32]

---

[29]Seumas Milne, "Scargill and the Spooks," *The Guardian*, November 19, 1994; Center for Democracy and Technology, "Domestic Intelligence Agencies: The Mixed Record of the UK's MI5," January 27, 2003.

[30]Quoted in Urban (1996, p. 48).

[31]RIPA also regulates the use of covert human intelligence sources and "directed surveillance" against intelligence targets. For more on this legislation, see Report of the Intelligence Services Commissioner for 2000, *Regulation of Investigatory Powers Act 2000, Chapter 23*, Cmnd. 5296, London: Her Majesty's Stationery Office, October 2001, and Home Office, *Covert Human Intelligence Sources: Code of Practice*, London: Her Majesty's Stationary Office, 2002.

[32]ISC (2002a, p. 5).

The ISC was an especially important development in terms of subjecting MI5 to an added layer of quasi-legislative oversight. The committee, which is made up of nine cross-party Members of Parliament (MPs), reports directly to the prime minister, operates within what is known as the "ring of secrecy," and is privy to some of the most highly classified information within the United Kingdom's national intelligence machinery.[33] It is obliged to produce an annual report on the overall performance of the British intelligence services, a "sanitized" version of which must be placed before Parliament for debate. In addition, the ISC conducts directed reviews and audits on an ad hoc basis, and, in 2003, it examined such high-profile topics as the October 2002 Bali bombings in Indonesia and the chain of events that led up to the Blair government's decision to go to war against Iraq in March 2003.[34]

---

[33]ISC (2003, p. 18); Cabinet Office (n.d., p. 23); "Committee Operates in Air of Secrecy," *Daily Telegraph*, June 4, 2003.

[34]"Spy Committee Will Investigate Blair," *The Glasgow Herald*, June 4, 2003; "Panel: Blair Was Warned About Risks," *Los Angeles Times*, September 13, 2003.

CHAPTER THREE

Security Intelligence in France

The Terrorist Threat

France currently faces no decisive domestic terrorist threat (with the exception of certain xenophobic right-wing groups connected with the National Front and regional separatists associated with Corsican and Basque extremism). The main danger confronting the country is that from international terrorist groups, especially those emanating from Islamist militants based in Algeria and other Maghreb countries. Such organizations as the Armed Islamic Group (GIA) and the Salafist Preaching and Combat Group (SPCG)—both of which act as associate entities of al Qaeda—are known to have established operational cells in France, benefiting from the country's sizable Muslim population (5 million out of 60 million total) and general geographic proximity to North Africa. The thrust of domestic counterterrorism intelligence is, accordingly, aimed at this particular threat contingency.

La Direction de la Surveillance du Territoire

The Direction de la Surveillance du Territoire (Directorate of Territorial Security, or DST) serves as France's main internal intelligence agency in terms of mitigating domestic threats from external sources. The bureau, which was created in 1944 and sits in the Ministry of the Interior, is charged with detecting and preventing activities inspired, engaged, or supported by hostile foreign powers or entities likely to threaten the safety and security of the country. Three main missions fall under this general mandate: (1) counterterrorism, which is the responsibility of the Central Intelligence Directorate; (2) counterespionage, which is the responsibility of the Counterespionage Sub-Directorate; and (3) the protection of France's economic and scientific infrastructure, which is the responsibility of the Economic Security and Protection of National Assets Department.

The DST relies on four main information collection methods in carrying out its counterterrorism role:

Informers. The DST runs an extensive network of informers who have been established or placed within the French Muslim community. In many instances, these insiders are convicted terrorist felons who have gained amnesty in exchange for cooperating with police and the security services. Gaining human-sourced intelligence in this way is something that is specifically sanctioned by the Vigipirate program,[1] which forms the basic structure of the French counterterrorism plan.

Community-Sourced Information. In addition to insiders, there is considerable emphasis on information provided by the general community. To facilitate this effort, the DST works with state authorities to develop integrated media campaigns explaining the purpose of counterterrorism measures and why they are being directed against certain groups and causes.

Monitoring Activities. Finally, the DST actively monitors immigrants entering France, especially those with an Islamic or North

---

[1]The basic structure of French counterterrorism is formed by the Vigipirate program, which was first enacted in 1986. This initiative outlines the jurisdictional parameters and procedures of the various agencies and departments involved in stemming and responding to offenses related to individual or collective attacks "aimed at disturbing the public order by means of intimidation or terror." The scope of the program was enhanced following the emergence of the GIA in the 1990s and has been further developed in the wake of al Qaeda's 9/11 attacks.

African background. All noncitizens are required to carry an identity card, and French nationals running hotels and guesthouses must inform authorities of the arrival and departure of any immigrants to whom they provide lodging. In addition, a centralized database has been created to document the names, addresses, and workplaces of irregular migrants—that is, those lacking proper documentation.[2] Combined, these various tracking measures provide the DST with an effective internal monitoring mechanism that can be brought to bear against terrorist sympathizers, activists with no prior criminal record, and extremists who manage to pass undetected through external immigration controls.

Foreign-Sourced Data. In addition to the domestic conduits above, the DST receives information provided by the Direction General de la Securité Exterieure (DGSE)—the country's external spy service. Over the past decade, the DST has been especially interested in intelligence pertaining to the overseas activities of the GIA, particularly those taking place in Algeria and the Maghreb, which have generally been directly targeted toward the perpetration of terrorism on French soil.

Raw intelligence data feed directly into domestic threat assessments and associated programs for physical protection and hardening. The institution of these measures is designed to be deliberately flexible, allowing specific plans to be upgraded or downgraded according to the situation at hand. Potential vulnerabilities are measured on the basis of the technical, organizational, and financial requirements needed to exploit them relative to the known capabilities and tactical preferences of groups operating in France.[3] The aim is not to prevent

---

[2]The identity of these irregulars is largely derived from an earlier immigration decree designed to regularize the status of any migrant expressing, in the form of a written application, a readiness and desire to formally integrate into French society. See "France: New Immigration Law," *Statewatch*, Vol. 8, No. 2, March/April 1998.

[3]Following the GIA attacks against the Paris metro in 1995, France instituted a seven-level plan of physical counterterrorism protection, the main parameters of which currently remain in force. These include

attacks from occurring under any circumstances (which is essentially impossible, particularly in open societies that do not unduly restrict freedom of movement and access); rather it is to protect targets and venues gauged to be at greatest risk and ensuring that if an act of terrorism does occur, it will not be repeated (as far as possible).[4]

In the event of a terrorist event occurring in France, the DST would immediately provide the police and investigating magistrates (see below) with the identity of all known militants, activists, and sympathizers in the country to avail "mopping up" arrests. These postincident detentions are designed to dry up the pool of active and passive support that foreign-based extremists need to sustain a viable operational tempo.

The DST and the Police

The DST maintains an extremely close working relationship with French law enforcement. The directorate collaborates with two main agencies in conducting surveillance over immigrant communities and formulating vulnerability risk assessments for general terrorist mitigation purposes (collectively enshrined under the framework of the Vigipirate program): the National Police (Direction Generale de la Police Nationale), which exercises jurisdiction in large urban areas and falls under the auspices of the Ministry of the Interior, and the National Gendarmerie (Direction Generale de la Gendarmerie), which is responsible for small towns and rural areas and falls under the jurisdiction of the Ministry of Defence.

Interaction between the DST and the police is largely instituted through the Anti-Terrorism Coordination Unit (Unité de Coordina-

---

- the institution of no-stop zones around prominent government buildings
- the division of the greater Paris metropolitan area into inner and outer rings, which are used to filter and control the number of trucks (and potential vehicular bombs) entering the capital's inner-city precincts
- close surveillance of "soft targets," such as schools and community centers, both of which have been a favored target of the GIA and foreign Islamists
- the deployment of armed police and gendarmes around public buildings, airports, and railway stations.

[4]Interview, French intelligence, Paris, April 28, 2001.

tion de la Lutte Anti-Terroriste, or UCLAT), a working level coordination group that includes agencies from the ministries of Interior and Defence. An additional structure, known as the Domestic Security Council, has also been created to facilitate communication flows between the intelligence and law enforcement communities.[5] It is expected that this body will form an important adjunct to UCLAT and be used to augment overall French antiterrorist contingencies in the post-9/11 environment.

In addition to the police, the DST shares an intimate relationship with investigating magistrates (*juge d'instruction*)—a small core of legal professionals who focus exclusively on various aspects of the terrorist phenomenon and who, in many ways, constitute the sharp end of the French judicial response to political extremism.[6] Their roles being described as a cross-section between a prosecutor and judge, these officials do not act as an advocate for prosecution or defense lawyers per se; rather, they are charged with conducting impartial, pretrial investigations to determine whether crimes of a terrorist nature have been committed. Because the magistrates are intended to act as nonbiased arbiters, they are granted fairly wide powers to open inquiries, authorize search warrants, issue subpoenas, and determine what constitutes an act (or the intent to commit an act) of terrorism. Over time, this latitude has effectively availed the emergence of a judicial intelligence service that has worked hand in

---

[5]Alain Faupin, "Reform of the French Intelligence Services After the End of the Cold War," paper presented before the Workshop on Democratic and Parliamentary Oversight of Intelligence Services, Geneva, October 3–5, 2002, p. 4; GAO, *Combating Terrorism: How Five Countries Are Organized to Combat Terrorism*, April 2002.

[6]The investigative magistrates characteristically specialize in cases related to specific classes of terrorism, such as separatist, ideological, and religious. The system has been able to develop due largely to the mutual confidence that has been forged between the intelligence services and specific personalities, such as Jean-Louis Bruguiere and Jean-Francois Ricard—both of whom have great experience in understanding Islamist networks and whose personal interactions with the DST have counted for a great deal.

glove with the DST in terms of extremist threat mitigation and pre-emption.[7]

DST Oversight and Accountability

No separate parliamentary system of intelligence scrutiny exists in France. Accountability is provided through the Ministry of the Interior and is largely viewed as an ongoing, routine function of agency management instituted through the Interministerial Liaison Committee Against Terrorism (Comité Interministériel de Lutte Anti-Terroriste, or CILAT).[8] This high-level body is empowered to establish ad hoc investigative commissions in the event that problems are found but does not act as a conduit to the national legislature for the purposes of independent intelligence oversight.[9]

The lack of parliamentary control in France, which is largely unique among Western democracies, is very much indicative of the country's political structure and the degree of discretion that it conveys across many areas of governance. Moreover, as Alain Faupin observes, it is also a legacy of history that reflects past connections between the French Communist Party and the Soviet Union:

> The reasons behind the absence of almost any parliamentary control over the intelligence services are perhaps to be found in the close connections that the French Communist Party, beginning in the 1920s, have striven to maintain with the Soviet Union . . . . Even if it was never in a position to lead the government, its presence, closely connected with our Cold War enemy, led the successive heads of the governments of the 4th

---

[7]Jeremy Shapiro and Benedicte Suzan, "The French Experience of Counter-Terrorism," *Survival*, Vol. 45, No. 1, 2003, p. 78. See also Gerard Chaliand, *L'arme du terrorisme*, Paris: Louis Audibert, 2002.

[8]CILAT also acts as a central coordinating mechanism for counterterrorism and is located within the Ministry of the Interior.

[9]GAO (2002, pp. 5, 15–16). It should be noted that France does have an independent government audit organization: the Court of Accounts (Cour des Comptes); however, it has not traditionally focused on intelligence and/or counterterrorism-related issues.

and 5th Republics, from the socialist party to the right wing, to deny Parliament any degree of control over these services.[10]

There have been moves to institute a more definitive structure of parliamentary control for the domestic and foreign intelligence services in France. One of the more notable initiatives in this regard is a project developed by Paul Quiles and Arthur Paecht that envisages the creation of a two-tier intelligence oversight mechanism with representation in each chamber of the national legislature. The intended purpose of such a body would be to provide the security services with an effective system of communication and accountability that would lend greater transparency to both the nature of their work and the specific requirements of their operational needs.[11] At the time of writing, however, no moves had been made to translate the Quiles-Paecht proposal into concerted policy action.

---

[10]Faupin (2002, p. 6).

[11]For further details, see Paul Quiles et al., *Proposition de loi tendant a la creation d'une delegation parliamentaire pour les affaires de renseignement*, Parliamentary document no. 1497, December 2, 1999.

CHAPTER FOUR

Security Intelligence in Canada

The Terrorist Threat

Canada has been largely free of indigenously based terrorism, with the main manifestations of current domestic political extremism restricted to sporadic and largely symbolic acts of environmental or animal-rights violence and protest.[1] However, the country has been decisively affected by the spillover effects of overseas conflicts and continues to act as a highly important hub of political, financial, and logistical support for Sikh and Islamic religious radicalism as well as ethno-nationalist separatist movements in Sri Lanka, Turkey, Ireland, and the Middle East. Over the past decade, terrorists linked to Hamas, Hizbollah, Egyptian Islamic Jihad, the GIA, al Qaeda, PIRA, the Kurdish Worker's Party (PKK), the Liberation Tigers of Tamil Eelam (LTTE), Babbar Khalsa, and the Dashmesh Regiment are known to have entered Canada—generally posing as refugees—to engage in various front and organizational support activities. Principal pursuits have included fund-raising, lobbying, weapon procurement, diaspora mobilization, money laundering, and people or commodity transit.[2]

---

[1]Typical acts have included tree spiking, economic sabotage, the spraying of noxious substances in public places, the mailing of letters containing razorblades, and, occasionally, pipe bombings and publicized threats of food poisoning.

[2]CSIS, "Counter-Terrorism," *Backgrounder Series*, No. 8, August 2002b, p. 6.

With the possible exception of the United States and the United Kingdom, there are more international terrorist organizations currently active in Canada than anywhere else in the world. To a large extent this situation owes itself to the fact that the country, which has been built on immigration and a commitment to ethno-nationalist and religious tolerance, represents a source of political refuge that has been effectively used by both peace-abiding and extremist elements from around the globe. It is toward the mitigation of the latter that the bulk of Canadian counterterrorism intelligence is directed.[3]

The Canadian Security Intelligence Service

Responsibility for domestic counterterrorism intelligence in Canada falls to the Canadian Security Intelligence Service (CSIS), which was created by an Act of Parliament (Bill C-9) on June 21, 1984. Prior to this, sole discretion for the collection of information related to domestic security rested in the hands of the Royal Canadian Mounted Police (RCMP), which exercised its function on the basis of a cabinet directive that essentially precluded any provision for independent oversight and control. The decision to run intelligence in this manner stemmed from emergency legislation relating to the crisis in the late 1960s and early 1970s with the Front de Liberation du Quebec (FLQ), whose campaign of bombings and kidnappings remains the most violent period of civil unrest in Canadian history.[4]

---

[3]Interview, CSIS, Ottawa, December 9, 2002.

[4]The FLQ was founded in 1963 by mainly left-wing militant French Canadians seeking the independence of Quebec. During the 1960s, the group took to bombing industrial premises and the political meetings of the country's ruling Liberal Party. Matters came to a head in October 1970 with the twin kidnappings of Richard Cross (UK trade commissioner) and Pierre Laporte (Canada's minister of labour and immigration). In response, the Trudeau government implemented the War Measures Act, which gave sweeping powers to the RCMP and army to enforce domestic security. Laporte was murdered on October 17; Cross was eventually freed on December 3, after his kidnappers were guaranteed free passage out of Canada to Cuba. See George Rosie, *The Directory of International Terrorism*, Edinburgh, UK: Mainstream Publishing, 1986, pp. 122–123.

By the early 1980s, however, there were mounting concerns that vesting a nonaccountable intelligence function within a domestic police agency that retained full powers of arrest threatened the democratic ethos of the Canadian way of life—particularly the right of all citizens to exercise legitimate political dissent. More specifically, there were fears that, if left unchecked, the RCMP could degenerate into a rogue agency under which the pretext of the national interest would be used to justify political surveillance. It was thus decided to create an entirely new, civilian intelligence organization—CSIS—that would have no ability to detain or apprehend suspects and which would have both a solid legal basis and an accompanying system of parliamentary checks and balances.[5]

CSIS is empowered to forewarn and advise government through the provision of timely and accurate information about activities that may constitute a direct threat to the domestic security of Canada. When CSIS was created in 1984, counterintelligence consumed 80 percent of the service's resources and efforts, with counterterrorism making up the remaining 20 percent. The growing prominence, lethality, and complexity of extremist violence since the end of the Cold War, and more particularly during the past five years, has caused this ratio to tilt substantially toward counterterrorism, making public safety the current number one priority of the service.[6]

Substantively, the bulk of CSIS activity is split into four main functional areas.[7] First and most fundamentally, a dedicated Threat Assessments Unit prepares and disseminates time-sensitive evaluations

---

[5]Interview, CSIS, Ottawa, December 9, 2002. See also CSIS, "The CSIS Mandate," *Backgrounder Series*, No. 1, August 2001, pp. 1–4, and FAS, "Royal Canadian Mounted Police (RCMP)," webpage, www.fas.org/irp/world/canada/rcmp/index.html.

[6]The proportion between counterterrorism and counterintelligence is now roughly 60/40. In fiscal year 2003, projected financial allocations to cover the war on terrorism are expected to amount to roughly C$155 million. For further details, see CSIS, *2001 Public Report*, Ottawa: Supply and Services Canada, 2002c, pp. 17–19.

[7]It should be noted that responsibility for security screening and vetting as well as front-end screening of applicants for refugee, immigrant, and citizenship status also falls to CSIS. In 2001, the service reviewed a total of 69,448 immigration cases and 163,858 citizenship applications, more than three times the number in the mid-1990s.

about the scope and immediacy of terrorist threats posed by groups and individuals in Canada. Second, case officers conduct interviews within local communities to explain the work of the intelligence services, to assess the likelihood of violence taking place in response to international political developments, and to determine which particular ethno-nationalist and religious groupings are more risk-prone than others. Third, CSIS provides input to the Enforcement Information Index, an automated database administered by Immigration and Customs that puts out alerts on known and suspected terrorists who may seek entry into Canada. Finally, the service works closely with other government departments and agencies at the federal, provincial, and municipal level to coordinate counterterrorist response activities in connection with threats and incidents.[8]

CSIS and the Police

Prior to 9/11, CSIS links with the police were essentially defined in terms of a bilateral relationship with the RCMP, which retained exclusive authority for investigating all crimes coming under the auspices of the CSIS Act or otherwise having clear implications for national security, including terrorism. Since the attacks on the World Trade Center and the Pentagon, however, the ambit of CSIS-police ties has been somewhat extended to include municipal forces as well as provincial units in Quebec and Ontario (neither of which contract out their policing function to the RCMP).[9] Three interrelated factors account for this extension:

1. Terrorism now falls under the penal jurisdiction of the Criminal Code of Canada, enforcement of which is the responsibility of local and provincial police forces.

---

[8]CSIS (2002b, pp. 8–11).

[9]The RCMP has entered into policing contracts with eight of Canada's provinces (Alberta, British Columbia, Saskatchewan, the Manitoba, Newfoundland, Nova Scotia, Winnipeg, and New Brunswick), two territories (Yukon and the Northwest Territories), and 201 (out of 571) municipalities.

2. Comprehensive counterterrorist investigations frequently require resources (technical and human) far beyond those that the RCMP can realistically supply.

3. Many of Canada's domestic terrorist problems are located in the country's larger metropolitan centers and cities—particularly Toronto, Montreal, and Vancouver—given their multicultural and multiracial diversity.[10]

CSIS places considerable importance on maintaining an effective working relationship with the police, largely because the agency has no powers of arrest of its own. Intelligence is shared with the RCMP and local or provincial forces when strategic evaluations indicate that a crime has occurred or is likely to occur. To facilitate the exchange of data and the formulation of accurate and up-to-date assessments, established liaison and secondment arrangements are maintained between CSIS and the RCMP, which are instituted on both a permanent and an ad hoc, as-needed basis. In addition, the service runs several regional suboffices to expedite information flows and associated "outreach" initiatives with local and provincial forces across the country.[11] Intelligence and police liaison is also a central feature of the Integrated National Security Assessment Centre (INSAC), an interagency information collection and analysis branch set up in 2003 to provide "single voice" assessments for Canadian counterterrorism purposes.[12] Finally, close CSIS–RCMP ties are provided through the National Counter-Terrorism Plan (NCTP), which provides a central mechanism for coordinating Canadian response measures in connection to extremist threats and incidents. By the end

---

[10]Interview, CSIS, Ottawa, December 9, 2002.

[11]Interview, CSIS, Ottawa, December 9, 2002.

[12]INSAC is mandated to assist in the prevention and disruption of national security threats at the earliest possible stage, thereby weakening threat infrastructures and preempting future threat-related activities. The centre draws on personnel on loan from throughout the Canadian security and intelligence communities, including representatives from defence, immigration, customs, transport, communications, critical infrastructure, foreign affairs, domestic intelligence, and law enforcement. For further details, see CSIS, "Integrated National Security Assessment Centre," *Backgrounder Series*, No. 13, October 2003.

of 2001, CSIS had delivered more than 800 briefings to law enforcement and other agencies under NCTP auspices.[13]

CSIS Oversight and Accountability

The legal basis for the operation of CSIS is provided by the Canadian Security Intelligence Service Act, which establishes two main oversight bodies for the agency: the Security and Intelligence Review Committee (SIRC), which answers directly to Parliament and is staffed along partisan lines representing all the main political and provincial interests in Canada, and the Executive Directorate of the Inspector General (EDIG), which reports to the Deputy Solicitor General (referred to as the Deputy Minister in the CSIS Act) or any person acting on his or her behalf. Both the SIRC and the EDIG exercise their oversight function in a largely similar manner, fulfilling two main roles: carrying out audits of CSIS and investigating complaints made against the service's officers. More specifically, the CSIS Act outlines the combined oversight responsibilities of the SIRC and the EDIG as the following:

- reviewing generally the performance by the service of its duties and functions
- arranging for additional reviews to be conducted, or conducting reviews of the service pursuant to relevant clauses of the CSIS Act
- conducting investigations in relation to complaints made against CSIS or its case officers
- monitoring, reviewing, and certifying the operational policies of CSIS.[14]

In addition to the EDIG and SIRC, the Federal Court of Canada exercises limited judicial control over CSIS, remaining the only

---

[13]CSIS (2002b, p. 10).

[14]See CSIS, *Canadian Security Intelligence Service Act*, R.S. 1985 C-23, March 2002a, chapters III.29 and III.38.

entity that can authorize a warrant allowing the service to use such intrusive investigative techniques as phone intercepts. Obtaining approval is itself the end product of a long and intensive decision-making process consisting of the following steps. First, CSIS must issue an affidavit that justifies the need for the specific measure in question. This submission is then reviewed by a senior committee within the service made up of the director and department managers in addition to external representatives from the Department of Justice and the Department of the Solicitor General. If the committee decides to proceed with the warrant application, the affidavit is forwarded to the Solicitor General for his or her personal consideration. Only once the document receives official approval at this stage is the Federal Court brought in to offer a final judgment on the validity and appropriateness of the initial CSIS request.[15]

---

[15]CSIS, "Accountability and Review," *Backgrounder Series*, No. 2, January 1996, pp. 2–3.

CHAPTER FIVE

Security Intelligence in Australia

The Terrorist Threat

Australia has been largely free of domestic and imported terrorism[1] and still does not confront the same level of threat as do other states in North America and Western Europe. This being said, the country's overall risk profile has been substantially heightened as a result of several developments over the past five years. Notably, these include Prime Minister John Howard's close alliance with the United States (which represents a reversal from previous Prime Minister Paul Keating's emphasis of engagement with Asia); his government's hosting of such prominent international events as the 2000 Olympic Games and the 2002 Commonwealth Heads of Government Meeting (or CHOGM); its lead role in the 1999–2000 East Timor intervention force (or INTERFET), which generated enormous opposi-

---

[1]To date, the most significant act of domestic terrorism to have taken place in Australia was the 1978 Hilton bombing in Sydney. Although mystery and conspiracy theories surround the attack (which left three people dead and eight injured), most informed observers believe it was connected to the Ananda Marga, a religious and spiritual sect seeking to assassinate Indian Prime Minister Morarji Desai in retaliation for the arrest of the group's charismatic leader, Prabhat Rainjan Sarkar (otherwise known as "Baba"). For an interesting account of the episode, see "Is This Man the Hilton Bomber?" *The Weekend Australian*, February 8–9, 2003.

tion in Indonesia;[2] and the unstinted backing his administration has given to the post-9/11 war on al Qaeda.[3] At the same time, globalization and increased cross-border movements of people, money, and commodities have rendered redundant the traditional defense afforded to this part of the world by geographic distance.

Currently, the main threat to Canberra's internal security emanates from Islamic extremists connected with Jemaah Islamiya (JI), which is alleged to act as Osama bin Laden's main terror wing in Southeast Asia.[4] The group has already been implicated in the October 2002 Bali bombings (which left 90 Australian nationals dead) and the more recent attack on the Jakarta Marriott in August 2003, and it is known to have made contacts with individuals in several major cities across the island continent, including Melbourne, Brisbane, and Sydney. Moreover, a number of JI affiliates are on record for stating their intention to attack Australian interests, both on account of Howard's strategic ties with Washington and in revenge for the supposedly imperial and arrogant attitude his government adopted following the intervention in East Timor.[5] It is the mitigation of so-called foreign-influenced politically motivated violence that, accordingly, accounts for the bulk of the country's operational and analytical intelligence resources in terms of counterterrorism.

---

[2]For an overview of Australia's role in this intervention, see Peter Chalk, *Australian Foreign and Defense Policy in the Wake of the 1999/2000 East Timor Intervention*, Santa Monica, Calif.: RAND Corporation, MR-1409-SRF, 2001.

[3]Along with the United Kingdom, Australia has been the most forceful proponent of the United States' post-9/11 war on terrorism.

[4]JI aims to build localized *jemaah islamiyya* (literally, Islamic communities) as precursors to pure Islamic states that would eventually join to form one pan-regional caliphate—or Nusantara Raya—incorporating Malaysia, Indonesia, southern Thailand, the southern Philippines, and Brunei. See Republic of Singapore, "The Jemaah Islamiyah Arrests and the Threat of Terrorism," white paper, January 7, 2003. For a good overview of the historical evolution and current dynamics of Jemaah Islamiya, see ICG, *Jemaah Islamiya in Southeast Asia: Damaged but Still Dangerous*, report no. 63, August 2003.

[5]Interview, Strategic and Defence Studies Centre, Canberra, February 6, 2003.

The Australian Security Intelligence Organisation

The Australian Security Intelligence Organisation (ASIO) remains Australia's principal counterterrorist intelligence body. The agency was created in 1949 and derives its authority from the ASIO Act of 1979.[6] It has no powers of arrest—although a 2003 amendment to the ASIO Act has given the organization limited rights to detain and question suspects before a prescribed authority (see the Appendix)—and is solely concerned with collecting and analyzing information on threats to the country's internal security.[7]

ASIO describes its principal output as a "secure Australia for people and property, for government business and national infrastructure, and for special events of national and international significance."[8] In working to achieve this objective, the agency collects and receives raw intelligence from a variety of sources, which is then assessed, analyzed, and disseminated to the government, police, and Australian Intelligence Community at large.

Similar to ASIO's counterparts—MI5, the DST, and CSIS—a considerable component of this information is derived from human sources. A small amount of these data emanate from well-placed "insiders" who may be either paid informants or plea bargainers. While this particular form of HUMINT is often the most valuable in terms of prioritizing targets for covert surveillance and/or gaining preemptive warnings of actual or latent threats to internal security, recruiting and training insiders for the purpose of counterterrorism is a time-consuming and expensive task. For this reason, the agency relies far more heavily on community-based information, most of which is obtained from direct interviews of local leaders and representatives. These meetings take place in both declared and undeclared

---

[6]See ASIO, *Report to Parliament 2001–2002*, Canberra: Commonwealth of Australia, 2002.

[7]Interviews, ASIO, Canberra, February 7, 2003, and the University of British Columbia, Vancouver, July 17, 2003.

[8]Parliamentary Joint Committee on ASIO, ASIS and DSD, *Annual Report 2001–2002*, Canberra: Parliament of the Commonwealth of Australia, 2002b, p. 17.

contexts (in the former, an ASIO affiliation is specifically acknowledged; in the latter, it is not) and focus on identifying and delineating municipal and regional developments that could affect, or otherwise have relevance for, national threat contingencies.[9]

Open-source information together with data gleaned from search, entry, and surveillance operations form an important adjunct to HUMINT. ASIO makes use of a wide variety of unclassified publications and assessments, including academic analyses, media reports, Internet-based documents, and conference papers and proceedings, to both augment general understanding of the global and strategic environment and assist in the development of operational responses to emerging security threats.

In addition, the agency actively collects information via computer access, intercepts of mail and telecommunications, and through covert listening and tracking devices. All of ASIO's work in this latter regard has to be sanctioned by the Attorney General and can only proceed after a warrant has been issued specifying the exact conditions governing the intrusive technique in question.[10]

Finally, and in common with agencies in the United Kingdom and France, ASIO has come to increasingly rely on data provided by other members of the national intelligence community—notably the Australian Secret Intelligence Service (ASIS, the country's external intelligence agency), the Defence Signals Directorate (DSD, the equivalent of GCHQ in the United Kingdom), and the Office of National Assessments (ONA, a strategic intelligence think tank that reports directly to the Prime Minister's Office). This supplementary source of information has been extremely important in terms of developing comprehensive threat assessments for such entities as JI, a group whose primary base of operations lies outside Australia's territorial boundaries but whose evolving actions are nevertheless

---

[9]Interview, ASIO, Canberra, February 7, 2003.

[10]ASIO (2002, pp. 37–39).

generally accorded to have direct relevance to the country's internal security environment.[11]

Following the increased publicity accorded to counterterrorism in the wake of 9/11 and—at least in Australia's case—the October 2002 Bali bombings, ASIO has moved to increase public understanding and awareness of its role in safeguarding internal security. A dedicated media liaison office now works in conjunction with major news, television, and radio networks and, through regular broadcast information messages, has moved to provide greater clarity about the legality, propriety, and effectiveness of the agency's work.[12]

These efforts have helped to offset the veil of secrecy that has traditionally surrounded ASIO, which has, in turn, availed greater public trust and confidence in working with the intelligence service. Reflecting this, communities around Australia provided more than 5,000 voluntary submissions to ASIO in 2002, directly responding to the government's call for a public that is "alert but not alarmed."[13] According to one official in Canberra, these solicitations played an important role in terrorism threat mitigation throughout the year and were particularly useful in augmenting general security planning and contingencies during the run-up to the 2002 CHOGM in Brisbane.[14]

ASIO and the Police

Similar to its counterparts in the United Kingdom, France, and Canada, ASIO relies heavily on cooperative relationships with law

---

[11]Interview, ASIO, Canberra, February 7, 2003.

[12]ASIO (2002, p. 49).

[13]ASIO (2002, pp. 15–16). The "be alert but not alarmed" message has been a central component of the Howard government's campaign to heighten public awareness of potential terrorist threats to Australian national security in the post-9/11 era. During February 2003, terrorism awareness packages were sent to every house in Australia, providing general background information on ASIO's counterterrorism program and how the public at large could assist in national contingency efforts.

[14]Interview, ASIO, February 7, 2003.

enforcement (federal, state, and local) to advance investigations into terrorist suspects and other persons of security interest. Most of these partnerships are established on the basis of agreed-upon memorandums of understanding, which typically cover a range of protocols pertaining to intelligence support, technical assistance, and training.[15]

The most-concerted links are with the Australian Federal Police (AFP), the rough equivalent of the FBI in the United States and the RCMP in Canada and the main agency responsible for enforcing law against crimes that have a specific national dimension. Like the Met in the United Kingdom, the AFP also reflects the Australian perspective on policing, especially in relation to matters that directly threaten or impinge on the country's domestic security (defined as terrorism, transnational crime, money laundering, major fraud, illicit drug trafficking, and electronic or cyber crime).[16]

Most AFP-ASIO interaction is conducted through the former's Transnational Crime Coordination Centre (formerly known as the National Assessments Centre), which provides a 24-hour point of contact for collaboration with state (and overseas) police forces as well as the intelligence services. A National Threat Assessment Centre, established in 2003 at ASIO headquarters in Canberra and including representation from the broader national security community, will form an important additional forum for police-intelligence interaction.[17] The AFP and ASIO also enjoy well-established liaison and data-sharing arrangements between their respective operational units

---

[15]Interview, Strategic and Defence Studies Centre, Canberra, February 6, 2003.

[16]AFP, "Our Role and Functions," webpage, www.afp.gov.au/page.asp?ref=/AboutAFP/Role Functions.xml.

[17]NTAC is mandated to prepare assessments of the likelihood and probable nature of terrorism (and other acts of politically motivated violence) against Australia, Australian citizens (at home and abroad), and Australian interests overseas. The center will initially include seconded officials from the AFP, ASIO, ASIS, ONA, Defence Intelligence Organisation, Department of Foreign Affairs and Trade, and the Department of Transport and Regional Services. A provision has been made to expand this representation at a later date should this prove necessary. For further details, see Department of the Attorney-General, "New Counter-Terrorism Intelligence Centre Launched," press release, October 17, 2003.

and, on a tactical level, benefit from high-level representation on several interagency coordinating cabinet bodies.[18] The more important of these bodies—all of which feed directly into national contingency plans for counterterrorism—include the following:

- National Counter-Terrorist Committee[19]
- Technical Support Unit[20]
- Counter-Terrorist Overseas Response Group.[21]

ASIO Oversight and Accountability

ASIO adheres to a range of accountability and safeguard arrangements that govern the way the agency operates. Principal structures and mechanisms of oversight include internal evaluation by the Attorney-General's Inspector-General of Intelligence and Security (IGIS) and external scrutiny performed through the Parliamentary Joint Committee (PJC) on ASIO, ASIS, and DSD.

The Inspector-General has wide-ranging powers and, unlike his or her counterpart in Canada, enjoys unlimited access to *all* organizational staff and documentation, including that pertaining to active operations. The IGIS may inquire independently into matters concerning ASIO legal compliance and propriety, at the request of the Attorney-General and/or the government or in response to com-

---

[18]Interview, ASIO, Canberra, February 7, 2003; AFP, "Australian Federal Police Counter Terrorism Measures," webpage, www.afp.gov.au/page.asp?ref=/International/LawEnforcement/CounterTerrorism.xml. These plans are formalized in the guise of the Australian National Counter-Terrorist Plan, which established the framework for coordinating the country's counterterrorism response.

[19]This committee acts as a centralized coordinating body that draws together a range of agencies concerned with counterterrorism. It was established in October 2002, largely to integrate and rationalize the work of the Standing Advisory Committee on Commonwealth/State Cooperation for Protection Against Violence and the Special Inter-Departmental Committee on Protection Against Violence.

[20]This unit provides technical intelligence support to state and federal police at the scene of a terrorist incident.

[21]This group is responsible for coordinating responses to overseas terrorist attacks or threats involving Australian nationals and/or interests.

plaints from the general public. Abridged outcomes of these investigations are compiled each year in the form of an annual report.

IGIS reviews of ASIO activity are extensive and can embrace any of the following substantive material and/or concerns:

- operational cases and files
- use of intrusive powers under warrant
- provision of information to, and liaison with, law enforcement
- official use of alternative documentation to support assumed identities
- access to and use of financial information obtained from the Australian Taxation Office and the Australian Transaction Reports and Analysis Centre.[22]

As noted above, an important feature of IGIS scrutiny is its ability to conduct real-time investigations into ongoing ASIO operational activities. This power ensures that the Inspector-General's oversight function is not merely ex post facto in nature and can be initiated at any time that some form of impropriety is suspected or otherwise judged to have taken place.[23]

The PJC—the main conduit for external ASIO review—was established as part of the September 2001 Intelligence Services Act, replacing the former Parliamentary Joint Committee on ASIO (PJCA).[24] The new structure has been vested with vastly expanded powers of intelligence oversight and is mandated to conduct investigations, either at its own behest or in response to a specific request from Parliament or the Attorney-General, into virtually all aspects of

---

[22]ASIO (2002, p. 47).

[23]Interview, ASIO, Canberra, February 7, 2003.

[24]The PJCA came into effect on August 31, 1988. Prior to this, there was no formal parliamentary scrutiny over the Australian intelligence community (and even after 1988, the remit of the PJCA was restricted to ASIO). See Parliamentary Joint Committee on ASIO, ASIS and DSD(2002b), pp. 2–4, and David MacGibbon, "Keeping an Eye on Our Watchers," *On Line Opinion*, September 1999.

ASIO administration and finance. It can request evidence and briefings from the agency's Director-General as well as serving case officers and is excluded only from material that is either operationally sensitive or relates to active intelligence-gathering priorities.[25] Unlike the former PJCA, PJC reviews must be undertaken at least once a year[26] and, because independent lines of inquiry can be initiated at any time, are not contingent on requests from outside third parties.[27]

---

[25]It should be noted that the PJC's remit also excludes reviews of individual complaints, responsibility for which is the exclusive domain of the IGIS.

[26]During its tenure, the PJCA conducted only four inquiries into ASIO, which were the subject of the following reports:

- *ASIO and the Archives Act* (April 1992)
- *ASIO and Security Assessment* (March 1994)
- *An Advisory Report on the Australian Security Intelligence Organisation Legislation Amendment Bill 1999* (May 1999)
- *A Watching Brief, The Nature, Scope and Appropriateness of ASIO's Public Reporting Activities* (September 2000).

[27]Parliamentary Joint Committee on ASIO, ASIS and DSD (2002b, pp. 1–9); ASIO (2002, pp. 47–48).

CHAPTER SIX

Assessment and Observations

Several aspects of the British, French, Canadian, and Australian models are worthy of note in terms of both strengths and weaknesses. While the experience of MI5, the DST, CSIS, and ASIO has been necessarily shaped by the particular political and security environment in which each has had to operate, it is possible to extrapolate positive and negative themes that are common across the four services and that, accordingly, would seem to have relevance beyond specific national contexts.

Strengths

On the positive side, at least eight observations stand out. First, all four countries vest domestic counterterrorism intelligence into the hands of dedicated agencies that have no functional law enforcement powers of arrest or detention. This has ensured the emergence of bureaus that are able to devote all their resources to preemptive information gathering, rather than the type of case-oriented investigations that necessarily characterize police-based intelligence units. Moreover, it has allowed for long-term surveillance of terrorist suspects (as intelligence services are not concerned with the immediate requirement of criminal prosecutions), which has helped with the disruption of both operational and/or logistical cells. Ultimately, the separation of security intelligence and law enforcement functions in these countries reflects what might be called a "culture of prevention" with respect to terrorism.[1] Indeed, each of the security services has long-term perspectives on the terrorist threat, and all have devoted substantial resources to honing analytical expertise, developing in-house foreign language skills, and becoming experts on their respective intelligence "targets."

Second, the United Kingdom, France, Canada, and Australia make extensive use of their intelligence services in local community information gathering. These activities have availed a useful "force multiplier" effect that has greatly enhanced the potential scope of national surveillance efforts. Moreover, because consistent media and information campaigns have frequently accompanied these initiatives, they have also helped to give the intelligence services more of a "public face" and at least provided a means to explain the nature, rationale, and purpose of their work.

One should not underestimate the "value added" dimension of this latter factor. Many British, French, Canadian, and Australian immigrants come from countries where internal security agencies have reputations for arbitrariness, brutality, and corruption. The natural inclination therefore has been to view the intelligence community with suspicion and largely bereft of concerns for civil rights and duties. Systematically moving to break down this negative perception has been vital in winning the trust of these communities and voluntarily gaining their solicitations for the furtherance of national security.

Third, a primary emphasis on the active recruitment and sourcing of terrorist insiders has consistently underscored the work of MI5 and the DST and, to a somewhat lesser extent, CSIS and ASIO. While the utility of electronic surveillance is certainly acknowledged, all four countries commonly view both its role in and contribution to counterterrorist operations as secondary to that of assessed and comprehensively analyzed HUMINT. As one intelligence official observes: "Human sources are the bread and butter of counterter-

---

[1]GAO (2002, p. 8).

rorism; you will never get a terrorist jumping out of a fiber optic cable."[2]

Framing overall data collection efforts in a human-sourced context has been highly effective in disrupting operational cells and providing high-grade intelligence on extremist intentions, capabilities, resources, and evolving dynamics. This has been evident in terms of British and French successes against al Qaeda and its affiliates, particularly the relative speed by which sleeper and operational cells have been rounded up post-9/11.[3]

HUMINT has also been integral to the time-sensitive threat assessments that British, Canadian, French, and Australian agencies produce on a regular basis and use to inform their respective police and policymaking communities. Just as importantly, it has contributed to well-developed physical protection programs, which has allowed for greater flexibility in target hardening while simultaneously helping to mitigate the wasteful and inefficient allocation of resources.

Fourth, the institution of comprehensive checks and balances has formed an integral component of the intelligence infrastructure in the Canadian, Australian, and, to a somewhat lesser extent, British cases. Reviews and audits conducted through the executive branch and at the parliamentary level have been integral to reviewing the operational activities of ASIO, CSIS, and MI5 and ensuring that their respective programs and resources are implemented in as effective, efficient, and legitimate a manner as possible.

The importance of these comprehensive structures of oversight cannot be stressed enough. By subjecting the otherwise secretive world of covert information gathering to independent scrutiny, they have provided a transparent medium through which to demonstrate the utility of the intelligence function in counterterrorism, to both politicians and the general public (in the form of annual reports). Just

---

[2]Interview, CSIS, Ottawa, December 9, 2002.

[3]Interviews, French intelligence, Paris, February 28, 2003, and Scotland Yard, London, June 3, 2003.

as importantly, they have helped to lend a degree of confidence that only balanced and controlled responses will be instituted in the name of national security and that these will not be used to unduly restrict individual rights and freedoms.

Fifth, the security intelligence agencies in each of these countries stress the importance of developing regular terrorist threat assessments that police forces as well industry can use to design viable and sustainable counterstrategies. These analyses have played a highly instrumental role in national counterterrorist planning in the four case study states concerned, all of which have only a limited suite of preventative capabilities to offset the extensive array of vulnerabilities that necessarily flow from their respective open societies. Certainly governments in London, Paris, Ottawa, and Canberra have come to appreciate the utility of rigorous assessments for augmenting general understanding of the nature and scope of the terrorist threat and thereby availing prudent decisionmaking about how best to allocate resources for future threat mitigation.[4]

Sixth, the United Kingdom, France, Canada, and Australia have all been able to draw on a wider, more diverse intelligence recruitment pool by stint of having internal security services that are not bounded or defined by the strictures of a domestic policing environment. This has been particularly important in terms of attracting individuals who would not normally be interested in entering a law enforcement profession, such as linguists, historians, economists, psychologists, social scientists, and those with established academic expertise in such areas as international relations, strategic studies, low-intensity conflict, and terrorism. The availability of these types of personnel has proven to be especially beneficial in terms of availing

---

[4]In 2002, the U.S. Justice Department's Office of the Inspector General noted that the FBI "has never performed a comprehensive written [analysis] of the risk of the terrorist threat facing the United States. Such an assessment would be useful not only to define the nature, likelihood, and severity of the threat but also to identify intelligence gaps that needed to be addressed" (Office of the Inspector General, *A Review of the Federal Bureau of Investigation's Counterterrorism Program: Threat Assessment, Strategic Planning, and Resource Management*, Report No. 02-38, September 2002). Recently, however, the bureau began developing a system for providing national threat assessments.

rounded, creative, and forward-looking analytical assessments that have straddled both the tactical and strategic dimensions of the so-called tasking, processing, exploitation, and dissemination chain.

Seventh, the existence of dedicated domestic security services in the United Kingdom, France, and Australia has helped to "smooth" information coordination with the foreign spy services in each of these countries—respectively, SIS, the DGSE, and ASIS.[5] While different jurisdictional mandates and responsibilities have obviously been extant (and, at times, problematic), common experience in an exclusive intelligence environment, combined with mutual recognition of the need for long-term, preemptive surveillance, has fostered a level of trust and understanding that has, in turn, fed into the development of viable bilateral counterterrorist data exchange arrangements. This has been of enormous importance in the modern era of "globalized terror," in which extremist threats to the national interest no longer accord to a neat internal-external dichotomy.

Finally, and in many ways following on from the previous point, divesting the intelligence function from law enforcement has necessarily meant that MI5, ASIO, CSIS, and the DST have had to operate in close tandem with their respective national police forces in terms of terrorist arrest, detention, and general threat mitigation. In all four cases, this has been achieved through the creation of dedicated coordinating bodies that have provided a central mechanism for disseminating information and availing interagency operations.[6]

Not only have these institutional forums allowed mutually beneficial relationships to emerge between the intelligence and police services in the United Kingdom, Australia, Canada, and France, they have also spurred the institution of wider integrated antiterrorism plans that have helped to offset problems associated with jurisdic-

---

[5]Canada has no separate overseas intelligence service of its own, relying primarily on information provided by friendly foreign services and bureaus.

[6]These bodies include the Police International Counter-Terrorism Unit, the National Joint Unit and Allied Matters Committee in the United Kingdom, the National Counter-Terrorism Committee in Australia; the Privy Council Office in Canada; and UCLAT and CILAT in France.

tional confusion and mismanagement. It is notable that in countries where police and intelligence responsibilities are vested under the aegis of a single agency—such as the FBI in the United States—rationalized response contingencies of this type have been comparatively late in developing (arguably because there has been less of a perceived need for the creation of wider organizational frameworks to cojoin separate security and law enforcement functions).

Weaknesses

It would be wrong, however, to suggest that the British, French, Canadian, and Australian models have not been without their problems. Difficulties have arisen in several areas relating to operational effectiveness and acceptability; information dissemination; and accountability.

Operational Effectiveness and Acceptability

Operationally, the counterterrorist track record of the four agencies has been far from perfect. CSIS has been consistently criticized for failing to adequately penetrate terrorist logistical cells that have been established on Canadian soil, generating widespread consternation in countries as diverse as India (with respect to Sikh extremists), Sri Lanka (with respect to the LTTE), Turkey (with respect to the PKK), and the United States (with respect to militants associated with Osama bin Laden).[7] More seriously, the service conspicuously failed to act on information provided by French intelligence that Ahmed Ressam, a resident Algerian national with links to al Qaeda and the GIA, was planning to carry out attacks in North America—a lapse

---

[7]"'Better Spies Needed Overseas'—Senator," *The National Post*, July 14, 1999; "Canada's Immigration Policies Face Criticism," *Los Angeles Times*, September 17, 2001; "Canada, U.S. Sign Pact on Terrorism," *New York Times*, December 14, 2001; "Canada Pledges to Tighten Border Controls," Reuters, February 29, 2000; "Spy Service Needs New Powers to Battle Terrorism," *The Globe and Mail*, January 15, 1999.

that almost resulted in the bombing of Los Angeles International Airport in December 1999.[8]

In the United Kingdom, MI5 has been accused of ignoring the threat posed by al Qaeda and remaining ignorant of the activities of Richard Reid—the so-called shoe bomber—who was neither questioned nor followed prior to his attempted suicide attack against an Air France airliner en route from Paris to Miami in late 2001.[9] Equally in Australia, regional analysts following the movements of JI charge ASIO blatantly disregarded threat assessments that, if followed, could have prevented the October 2002 Bali tragedy.[10]

Finally, despite scoring some notable successes against the GIA, the DST has not always been effective in dismantling parallel networks of Islamist militants, some of which have been associated with highly audacious attacks in France. A case in point was the wave of terrorist bombings that hit Paris between July 11 and October 17, 1995, which took the intelligence services by surprise and have since been tied to Algerian cells based in Lille and Lyon.[11]

Just as importantly, there have been several instances when accepted democratic norms and operational limits have been violated in the name of counterterrorism. MI5, for instance, has been directly embroiled in scandals involving the use of Special Air Service (SAS)

---

[8]Shapiro and Suzan (2003, p. 67); "The Terrorist Within," *Seattle Times*, 18-part series, June 22–July 8, 2002; "Canada, U.S. Sign Pact on Terrorism" (2001); "Canada's Immigration Policies Face Criticism" (2001). In the event, Ressam was apprehended trying to cross into Washington state on a ferry from British Columbia after an alert U.S. customs officer discovered a trunk load of explosives in his car.

[9]Center for Democracy and Technology (2003), p. 3; "MI5 Blunder Over Bomber," *The Observer*, December 30, 2001; "MI5 Accused of Ignoring Al-Qaeda," *The Scotsman*, June 20, 2002.

[10]Interviews, The Intelligence Corps, AFP, Sydney, May 23, 2003, and Institute of Defense and Strategic Studies, Singapore, September 10, 2003. See also "Canberra 'Ignored Facts on Indonesia,'" *The Age*, January 8, 2003.

[11]Shapiro and Suzan (2003, p. 80); "Jewish School Targeted in Car Bombing," *The Australian*, September 13, 1995; "Bomb Explosion in Paris Subway Kills 4, Injures 60," *Vancouver Sun*, July 26, 1995; "Algerian Militants Suspected in Blast," *Vancouver Sun*, July 28, 1995; "France Acts to Combat Bombers," *The Australian*, September 12, 1995; "Colonial Past Haunts France," *The Australian*, September 30, 1995.

and Royal Ulster Constabulary (RUC) undercover units to kill (rather than arrest) identified members of PIRA as well as the recruitment of active Protestant hit squads to carry out assassinations against leading Catholic paramilitaries and sympathizers.[12] The DST, working under the authority of investigating magistrates,[13] has frequently helped to direct mass roundups of alleged Islamic militants residing in France, many of whom had no known connection to terrorism and were detained only because they happened to be present at the time of police "mopping up" operations.[14] ASIO has similarly been criticized for arbitrary and indiscriminate practices, including past break-ins of left-wing academics holding "suspect" political affiliations or views and, since 9/11, the increasing resort to wiretaps and surveillance of the some 280,000 Muslims currently residing in Australia.[15]

Related to the above is the lowering of the "democratic threshold" that has tended to accompany the establishment of dedicated domestic intelligence agencies. Because these bodies are already vested with unique powers of covert surveillance and monitoring, they inevitably play an important role in "bureaucratically normalizing" state security infrastructures that have considerable authority over the indi-

---

[12]Center for Democracy and Technology (2003, p. 4); Leslie Macfarlane, "Human Rights and the Fight Against Terrorism in Northern Ireland," *Terrorism and Political Violence*, Vol. 4, No. 1, 1992; John Stalker, *Ireland, "Shoot to Kill" and the "Affair,"* Harmondsworth, UK: Penguin Books, 1988; "MI5 and Army Hindered Finucane Case," *The Independent*, June 24, 2002; "Truth, Lies and Steaknives," *The Economist*, May 17, 2003; "Army and Police Colluded in Killings," *The Weekend Australian*, April 19–20, 2003.

[13]In France, the DST can be placed under the authority of a magistrate, which essentially gives the agency a dual role as both an intelligence service and a judicial police force. See Shapiro and Suzan (2003, p. 82).

[14]Interview, *Statewatch*, London, November 26, 2001; Shapiro and Suzan (2003, pp. 84–85). Perhaps the clearest example of the policy at work followed the series of blasts on the Paris metro in summer 1995, when mass arrests of Algerians suspected of belonging to the Islamic Salvation Front and the GIA took place (in one raid, 170 individuals were detained). See "France: Anti-Terror Laws Pave Way for Arbitrary Justice," *Statewatch*, Vol. 9, Nos. 3–4, May–August 1999.

[15]"Australians Are Fast Becoming the Most Spied-On People in the Western World," *The Sunday Tasmanian*, June 29, 2003; "Tough on Muslims," *The Economist*, November 30, 2002.

vidual. The United Kingdom's MI5, for example, remains essentially "self-tasking," meaning that it requires no separate ministerial permission before initiating a new operation. In the words of one journalist who closely follows the agency, "the broad, if not open-ended, mandate to protect [the] national [interest] leave the service itself to decide what constitutes a security threat."[16] While this may not necessarily be problematic in and of itself—publics generally accept such official intrusion as a "necessary evil"—it can, under certain circumstances, encourage governments to contemplate unwarranted departures from customary civil-judicial practices.[17]

To an extent, this has already been evident in governments in the United Kingdom, Canada, and Australia, all of which have sought to expand the scope and remit of internal policing and intelligence gathering through post-9/11 antiterrorism legislation that has been criticized as unnecessarily harsh and intrusive. Areas that have generated particular concern include (1) the granting of enhanced powers to intercept and track emails, telephone calls, and Internet browsing; (2) the banning of inflammatory speeches (which, in the United Kingdom, can now be subjected to penalization under a new class of crime—"inciting religious hatred"); (3) the sanctioning of varying extrajudicial arrest and detention procedures (which in Australia's case extend, at least partially, to ASIO); (4) the watering down of accepted constitutional principles, such as "innocent until proven guilty"; (5) the increased provision for evidence of a closed, secret, or even coerced nature to be used in court; and (6) the annulment of access restrictions that have traditionally safeguarded such personal data as tax, bank, and health records.[18]

---

[16]Michael Smith, *New Cloak, Old Dagger: How Britain's Spies Came in from the Cold*, London: Victor Gollancz, 1996, p. 79.

[17]See, for instance, Peter Chalk, *West European Terrorism and Counter-Terrorism: The Evolving Dynamic*, London: Macmillan, 1996, chapter five.

[18]"Australians Are Fast Becoming the Most Spied-On People in the Western World" (2003); "Coming Quietly," *The Economist*, March 1, 2003; "Tough on Muslims" (2002); "Should Britons Be Interned Too?" *The Daily Telegraph*, October 31, 2002; "In Canada, a Sea Change Follows Wave of Terrorism," *Los Angeles Times*, January 28, 2002; "Canada's Terrorism Bill Raises Familiar Worries," *Washington Post*, December 3, 2001.

Information Dissemination

Difficulties have also been evident in terms of information dissemination. Both MI5 and CSIS have been accused of failing to pass on intelligence to relevant authorities that could have prevented several high-profile terrorist incidents, including, in the former's case, attacks against the Israeli Embassy in 1994 and London's Docklands in 1996, and, in the latter's, the bombing of an Air India Boeing 747 in 1985.[19] Equally, while ASIO frequently does coordinate its tactical and intelligence operations with the AFP, it is not obliged to do so and has, on occasion, deliberately withheld information on the basis of its own idiosyncratic calculation of the national interest. This caveat to bilateral working ties has caused some disquiet within the law enforcement community, eliciting a view that the ASIO-AFP relationship is neither two-way or, indeed, mutually beneficial. One former high-ranking federal police officer claims that this problem has steadily worsened since 2002 on account of jurisdictional jealousies arising over investigative visibility and profile that have been accorded the AFP in the wake of the Bali bombings.[20]

In common with the United States, the issue of trust has frequently been a major factor in mitigating the effective dissemination of information among and between counterterrorism agencies and bureaus. In Canada, CSIS has refrained from exchanging sensitive data with municipal and provincial police forces for fear that they will be made public in court or hearings before administrative tribunals.[21] In the United Kingdom, areas of friction have arisen between the Security Service and local SBs, particularly in instances in which MI5 case officers have moved to centrally sanitize intelligence gathered

---

[19]Center for Democracy and Technology (2003, p. 4); "Second Bomb in Two Days Rocks London," *Vancouver Sun*, July 27, 1994; "Middle Eastern–Inspired Mayhem in Britain," *The Sunday Times*, July 31, 1994; "MI5 Warned of IRA Bombing One Month Ago," *New York Times*, February 13, 1996; "Coverup by Canadian Spy Agency Alleged; Sikh Agent Reputedly Had Advanced Information About 1985 Airline Bombing" *Washington Post*, June 3, 2003.

[20]Interviews, Strategic and Defense Studies Centre and AFP, February 6, 2003.

[21]"New Laws Needed to Thwart Spies and Terrorists," *Vancouver Sun*, July 7, 1999.

from covert human sources employed in joint-owned operations.[22] And in France, coordination between the police and intelligence services has, at least historically, been subject to chronic problems of mistrust, with agencies not only failing to collaborate but moreover occasionally working at complete cross-purposes with one another.[23]

Accountability

Beyond operational and organizational matters, some fairly significant gaps in intelligence accountability and bureaucratic control have been apparent. In the United Kingdom, for example, while the ISC is composed of sitting parliamentarians, it is both appointed by and answers directly to the prime minister. Critics have decried this arrangement as offering only the "barest of fig leaves" in terms of comprehensive external scrutiny, arguing further that ministers and MPs existing outside the privileged ring of secrecy can never hope to know the true extent of MI5 operations.[24] Problems are even greater in France, where no legislative oversight exists. Given the close relationship between the DST and investigating magistrates, the absence of nonexecutive mechanisms of accountability can quickly translate into a carte blanche counterterrorist mandate that transcends across the operational and judicial spheres. As Shapiro and Suzan observe:

> Another frequent criticism [of the French system] is that there is no [separate] controlling authority over the anti-terrorism magistrates [and the DST] and that the scope of [current antiterrorist

---

[22]"Special Branch More Than Doubles in Size" (2003). Such tensions are not new. During World War I, for instance, MI5 and MPSB were locked in a bitter rivalry over counter-espionage operations. See Andrew (1987, p. 191).

[23]See, for example, Shapiro and Suzan (2003, p. 75).

[24] "Bugging Team" *The Guardian,* December 9, 1999; Richard Tomlinson, *The Big Breach: From Top Secret to Maximum Security*, Edinburgh, UK: The Cutting Edge Press, 2001, p. 8; Michael White and Patrick Wintour, "Old-Fashioned Committee Provides a Window on Whitehall's 'Ring of Secrecy,'" *The Guardian*, September 11, 2003.

legislation] offer[s] them excessive scope to decide what constitutes terrorism or intent to commit terrorism.[25]

---

[25]Shapiro and Suzan (2003, p. 85).

CHAPTER SEVEN
Conclusion

To be sure, significant differences exist between the United States on the one hand and the United Kingdom, France, Canada, and Australia on the other. From a historical standpoint, the French and British experience of subversion and terrorism has inured the publics in both states to an invasive intelligence and surveillance bureaucracy that would certainly be viewed as unacceptable in America—the events of September 11, 2001, notwithstanding. In addition, the case studies highlight the existence of administrative bureaucracies and police structures that are more centralized than those found in the United States (something that is particularly true in France and the United Kingdom), are characterized by parliamentary systems of government rather than a strict separation of powers, tend not to endorse gun ownership as an intrinsic right of the individual (and, hence, militias have not played a prominent role in the national realm), and are primarily regionally focused in terms of their broader economic, security, and political interests. These dichotomies necessarily mean that intelligence institutions cannot, and indeed should not, simply be replicated from one national context to the next—irrespective of their relative efficacy in their original setting.[1]

This being said, the United Kingdom, France, Canada, and Australia do share important defining characteristics with the United

[1]Shapiro and Suzan (2003, p. 88); Todd Masse, *Domestic Intelligence in the United Kingdom: Applicability of the MI-5 Model to the United States*, Washington, D.C.: Congressional Research Service, May 19, 2003, pp. 6–10; Ensum (2002, p. 102).

States, including, notably, (1) liberal democratic traditions and institutions, (2) a common concern with stemming threats to domestic stability through the institution of robust internal security infrastructures, and (3) acceptance of the need to balance operational effectiveness in the fight against terrorism with the concomitant need to respect fundamental norms integral to the effective functioning of an open society. These traits make it useful to consider how each of the countries has organized its respective counterterrorist capabilities, if only as a benchmark for guiding possible developments in the United States.

No less importantly, the four case studies highlight practical operational and organizational lessons that would be extremely valuable, and perhaps even necessary, in the event that a decision is made to create a dedicated domestic intelligence bureau in the United States.

The Australian Security Intelligence Organisation Legislation Amendment (Terrorism) Act, 2003: Background Information

The ASIO Act of 2003 is part of a suite of legislation introduced by the Howard government in the immediate aftermath of the September 11, 2001 terrorist attacks on the United States. It outlines proposed changes to the ASIO Act of 1979 designed to avail the collection of domestic intelligence that could be used to thwart acts of terrorism and/or gain the prosecution of those resorting to such measures.[1]

Specifically, the act empowers ASIO to obtain warrants from the Attorney-General that will sanction the right to detain, search, and question terrorist suspects before a prescribed authority of the state, who can be either a federal magistrate, a deputy president, or a legally qualified member of the Administrative Appeals Tribunal. These persons can be held for a maximum of seven days, after which they must either be charged or released. The act's provisions apply to persons 16 years and older and are currently subject to a three-year sunset clause.[2]

---

[1]See Parliamentary Joint Committee on ASIO, ASIS and DSD, *An Advisory Report on the Australian Security Intelligence Organisation Legislation Amendment (Terrorism) Bill 2002*, Canberra: Parliament of the Commonwealth of Australia, 2002a.

[2]Australian Human Rights and Equal Opportunities Commission, "Statement on the Australian Security Intelligence Organisation Legislation Amendment (Terrorism) Act," June 27, 2003.

Bibliography

Official Reports and Testimony

Advisory Panel to Assess Domestic Response Capabilities for Terrorism Involving Weapons of Mass Destruction (also known as the Gilmore Commission), *Fourth Annual Report to the President and the Congress of the Advisory Panel to Assess Domestic Response Capabilities for Terrorism Involving Weapons of Mass Destruction*, December 15, 2002.

AFP—*see* Australian Federal Police.

Australian Federal Police, "Australian Federal Police Counter Terrorism Measures," webpage, www.afp.gov.au/page.asp?ref-/International/Law Enforcement/CounterTerrorism.xml (accessed October 2003).

――――, "Our Role and Functions," webpage, www.afp.gov.au/page. asp?ref=/AboutAFP/RoleFunctions.xml (accessed October 2003).

Australian Security Intelligence Organisation (ASIO), *Report to Parliament 2001–2002*, Canberra: Commonwealth of Australia, 2002.

Cabinet Office (UK), *National Intelligence Machinery*, London: Her Majesty's Stationery Office, n.d.

――――, *The United Kingdom and the Campaign Against International Terrorism: Progress Report*, London: Her Majesty's Stationery Office, September 9, 2002.

――――, *Cabinet Office Departmental Report 2003*, Cmnd. 5926, London: Her Majesty's Stationery Office, May 2003.

Canadian Security and Intelligence Service, "Accountability and Review," *Backgrounder Series*, No. 2, January 1996.

_____, "The CSIS Mandate," *Backgrounder Series*, No. 1, August 2001.

_____, *Canadian Security Intelligence Service Act*, R.S. 1985 C-23, March 2002a.

_____, "Counter-Terrorism," *Backgrounder Series*, No. 8, August 2002b.

_____, *2001 Public Report*, Ottawa: Supply and Services Canada, 2002c.

_____, "Integrated National Security Assessment Centre," *Backgrounder Series*, No. 13, October 2003, www.csis-scrs.gc.ca/eng/menu/otherdocs_e.html (accessed December 2003).

CSIS—*see* Canadian Security Intelligence Service.

Department of the Attorney-General (Australian), "New Counter-Terrorism Intelligence Centre Launched," press release, October 17, 2003, www.asio.gov.au/Media/Contents/ntac_launched.htm (accessed November 2003).

FBI—*see* U.S. Federal Bureau of Investigation.

GAO—*see* U.S. General Accounting Office.

Her Majesty's Inspector of Constabulary (UK), *A Need to Know: HMIC Thematic Inspection of Special Branch and Ports Policing*, London: Home Office Communication Directorate, January 2003.

HMIC—*see* Her Majesty's Inspector of Constabulary.

Home Office (UK), "Terrorism: What We Face," webpage, www.home office.gov.uk/terrorism/threat/face/index.html (accessed October 2003).

_____, *Covert Human Intelligence Sources: Code of Practice*, London: Her Majesty's Stationery Office, 2002.

Home Office and Scottish Home and Health Department (UK), *Guidelines on Special Branch Work in Great Britain*, London, July 1994.

Intelligence and Security Committee (UK), *Annual Report 2001–2002*, Cmnd. 5542, London: Her Majesty's Stationery Office, June 2002a.

_____, *Inquiry into Intelligence, Assessments and Advice Prior to the Terrorist Bombings on Bali 12 October 2002*, Cmnd. 5724, London: Her Majesty's Stationery Office, December 2002b.

_____, *Annual Report 2002–2003*, Cmnd. 5837, London: Her Majesty's Stationery Office, June 2003.

ISC—*see* Intelligence and Security Committee.

Mueller, Robert S., III, "Progress Report on the Reorganization and Refocus of the FBI," testimony before the U.S. House of Representatives Committee on Appropriations, Subcommittee on the Departments of Commerce, Justice, and State, the Judiciary, and Related Agencies, June 18, 2003, www.fbi.gov/congress/congress03/mueller061803.htm (accessed October 2003).

Parliamentary Joint Committee on ASIO, ASIS and DSD, *An Advisory Report on the Australian Security Intelligence Organisation Legislation Amendment (Terrorism) Bill 2002*, Canberra: Parliament of the Commonwealth of Australia, 2002a.

———, *Annual Report 2001–2002*, Canberra: Parliament of the Commonwealth of Australia, 2002b.

Quiles, Paul, et al., *Proposition de loi tendant a la creation d'une delegation parliamentaire pour les affaires de renseignement*, Parliamentary document no. 1497, December 2, 1999.

Report of the Intelligence Services Commissioner for 2000 (UK), *Regulation of Investigatory Powers Act 2000, Chapter 23*, Cmnd. 5296, London: Her Majesty's Stationery Office, October 2001.

Republic of Singapore, "The Jemaah Islamiyah Arrests and the Threat of Terrorism," white paper, January 7, 2003.

Security Service (UK), *The Security Service: MI5*, 4th edition, London: Her Majesty's Stationery Office, n.d.

U.S. Congress, Senate Select Committee on Intelligence and House Permanent Select Committee on Intelligence, *Joint Inquiry into Intelligence Community Activities Before and After the Terrorist Attacks of September 11, 2001*, December 2002.

U.S. Federal Bureau of Investigation, *Terrorism in the United States: 1998*, U.S. Department of Justice, 1999.

U.S. General Accounting Office, *Combating Terrorism: How Five Countries Are Organized to Combat Terrorism*, April 2002.

U.S. Office of the Inspector General, *A Review of the Federal Bureau of Investigation's Counterterrorism Program: Threat Assessment, Strategic Planning, and Resource Management*, U.S. Department of Justice, report no. 02-38, September 2002, www.usdoj.gov/oig/audit/0238/exec.htm (accessed October 2003).

Books and Monographs

Andrew, Christopher, *Her Majesty's Secret Service: The Making of the British Intelligence Community*, New York: Penguin Books, 1987.

Chaliand, Gerard, *L'arme du terrorisme*, Paris: Louis Audibert, 2002.

Chalk, Peter, *West European Terrorism and Counter-Terrorism: The Evolving Dynamic*, London: Macmillan, 1996.

_____, *Australian Foreign and Defense Policy in the Wake of the 1999/2000 East Timor Intervention*, Santa Monica, Calif.: RAND Corporation, MR-1409-SRF, 2001.

Hollingsworth, Mark, and Nick Fielding, *Defending the Realm: MI5 and the Shayler Affair*, London: André Deutsch Limited, 1999.

Rimington, Stella, *Open Secret: The Autobiography of the Former Director-General of MI5*, London: Hutchinson, 2001.

Rosie, George, *The Directory of International Terrorism*, Edinburgh, UK: Mainstream Publishing, 1986.

Smith, Michael, *New Cloak, Old Dagger: How Britain's Spies Came in from the Cold*, London: Victor Gollancz, 1996.

Stalker, John, *Ireland: "Shoot to Kill" and the "Affair,"* Harmondsworth, UK: Penguin Books, 1988.

Tomlinson, Richard, *The Big Breach: From Top Secret to Maximum Security*, Edinburgh, UK: The Cutting Edge Press, 2001.

Urban, Mark, *UK Eyes Alpha: The Inside Story of British Intelligence*, London: Faber and Faber, 1996.

Independent Reports, Book Chapters, Journal Articles, and Conference Reports

Center for Democracy and Technology, "Domestic Intelligence Agencies: The Mixed Record of the UK's MI5," January 27, 2003, www.cdt.org/security/usapatriot/030127mi5.pdf (accessed October 2003).

Ensum, Joanna, "Domestic Security in the United Kingdom: An Overview," in Markle Foundation Task Force, *Protecting America's Freedom in the Information Age*, New York: Markle Foundation, October 2002.

Faupin, Alain, "Reform of the French Intelligence Services After the End of the Cold War," paper presented before the Workshop on Democratic and Parliamentary Oversight of the Intelligence Services, Geneva, October 3–5, 2002.

ICG—*see* International Crisis Group.

International Crisis Group, *Jemaah Islamiya in Southeast Asia: Damaged but Still Dangerous*, report no. 63, August 2003.

Macfarlane, Leslie, "Human Rights and the Fight Against Terrorism in Northern Ireland," *Terrorism and Political Violence*, Vol. 4, No. 1, 1992.

Masse, Todd, *Domestic Intelligence in the United Kingdom: Applicability of the MI-5 Model to the United States*, Washington, D.C.: Congressional Research Service, May 19, 2003.

Shapiro, Jeremy, and Benedicte Suzan, "The French Experience of Counter-Terrorism," *Survival*, Vol. 45, No. 1, 2003.

Wortzel, Larry M., "Americans Do Not Need a New Domestic Spy Agency to Improve Intelligence and Homeland Security," *Heritage Foundation Executive Memorandum*, No. 848, January 10, 2003.

Newspaper and Magazine Articles, Commentaries, and Information Sheets

"A Top Intelligence Post Goes to CIA Officer in Spy Case," *New York Times*, March 14, 2003.

"Algerian Militants Suspected in Blast," *Vancouver Sun*, July 28, 1995.

"Army and Police Colluded in Killings," *The Weekend Australian*, April 19–20, 2003.

Australian Human Rights and Equal Opportunities Commission, "Statement on the Australian Security Intelligence Organisation Legislation Amendment (Terrorism) Act," June 27, 2003, www.hreoc.gov.au/media/releases/2003/35_03.html (accessed October 2003).

"Australians Are Fast Becoming the Most Spied-On People in the Western World," *The Sunday Tasmanian*, June 29, 2003.

"'Better Spies Needed Overseas'—Senator," *The National Post* [Toronto], July 14, 1999.

"Bomb Explosion in Paris Subway Kills 4, Injures 60," *Vancouver Sun*, July 26, 1995.

"Bugging Team," *The Guardian* [London], December 9, 1999.

"Canada Pledges to Tighten Border Controls," Reuters, February 29, 2000.

"Canada, U.S. Sign Pact on Terrorism," *New York Times*, December 14, 2001.

"Canada's Immigration Policies Face Criticism," *Los Angeles Times*, September 17, 2001.

"Canada's Terrorism Bill Raises Familiar Worries," *Washington Post*, December 3, 2001.

"Canberra 'Ignored Facts on Indonesia,'" *The Age* [Melbourne], January 8, 2003.

"Colonial Past Haunts France," *The Australian*, September 30, 1995.

"Coming Quietly," *The Economist*, March 1, 2003.

"Committee Operates in Air of Secrecy," *Daily Telegraph* [London], June 4, 2003.

Corera, Gordon, "Report Points to Weaknesses in US Intelligence Machinery," *Jane's Intelligence Review*, September 2003.

"Coverup by Canadian Spy Agency Alleged; Sikh Agent Reputedly Had Advanced Information About 1985 Airline Bombing," *Washington Post*, June 3, 2003.

FAS—*see* Federation of American Scientists.

Federation of American Scientists (FAS), Intelligence Resource Program, "Royal Canadian Mounted Police [RCMP]," www.fas.org/irp/world/canada/rcmp/index.html (accessed October 2003).

"France Acts to Combat Bombers," *The Australian*, September 12, 1995.

"France: Anti-Terror Laws Pave Way for Arbitrary Justice," *Statewatch*, Vol. 9, Nos. 3–4, May–August, 1999.

"France: New Immigration Law," *Statewatch*, March/April 1998.

"In Canada, a Sea Change Follows Wave of Terrorism," *Los Angeles Times*, January 28, 2002.

"Is This Man the Hilton Bomber?" *The Weekend Australian*, February 8–9, 2003.

"Jewish School Targeted in Car Bombing," *The Australian*, September 13, 1995.

"Lawmakers Worry New Terrorist Threat Integration Center Is Just Another Layer of Bureaucracy," *All Things Considered* (National Public Radio), July 23, 2003.

MacGibbon, David, "Keeping an Eye on Our Watchers," *On Line Opinion*, September 1999, www.onlineopinion.com.au/Sep99/MacGibbon.htm (accessed October 2003).

Metropolitan Police (UK), "Specialist Operations," webpage, www.met.police.uk/so/index.htm (accessed October 2003).

"MI5 Accused of Ignoring Al-Qaeda," *The Scotsman* [Edinburgh], June 20, 2002.

"MI5 and Army Hindered Finucane Case," *The Independent* [London], June 24, 2002.

"MI5 Blunder Over Bomber," *The Observer* [London], December 30, 2001.

"MI5 Warned of IRA Bombing One Month Ago," *New York Times*, February 13, 1996.

"Middle Eastern–Inspired Mayhem in Britain," *The Sunday Times* [London], July 31, 1994.

Milne, Seumas, "Scargill and the Spooks," *The Guardian* [London], November 19, 1994.

"New Laws Needed to Thwart Spies and Terrorists," *Vancouver Sun*, July 7, 1999.

"No to an American MI5," *Washington Post*, January 5, 2003.

"Panel: Blair Was Warned About Risks," *Los Angeles Times*, September 13, 2003.

"Police Colluded in Killings," *The Weekend Australian*, April 19–20, 2003.

"Quiet Lives Hid a Quest to Recruit for Global Jihad," *Daily Telegraph* [London], April 2, 2003.

"Second Bomb in Two Days Rocks London," *Vancouver Sun*, July 27, 1994.

"Should Britons Be Interned Too?" *The Daily Telegraph* [London], October 31, 2002.

"Special Branch More Than Doubles in Size," *Statewatch*, September 2003.

"Spy Committee Will Investigate Blair," *Glasgow Herald*, June 4, 2003.

"Spy Service Needs New Powers to Battle Terrorism," *The Globe and Mail* [Toronto], January 15, 1999.

Taylor, Stuart, Jr., "Spying on Terrorists," *GovExec.com*, January 13, 2003, www.govexec.com/dailyfed/0103/011303ff.htm (accessed October 2003).

"The Terrorist Within," *Seattle Times*, 18-part series, June 22–July 8, 2002.

"Tough on Muslims," *The Economist*, November 30, 2002.

"Truth, Lies and Steaknives," *The Economist*, May 17, 2003.

White, Michael, and Patrick Wintour, "Old-Fashioned Committee Provides a Window on Whitehall's 'Ring of Secrecy,'" *The Guardian* [London], September 11, 2003.

About the Authors

Peter Chalk is a policy analyst with the RAND Corporation, Santa Monica, Calif. He is also associate editor of *Studies in Conflict and Terrorism* and an adjunct professor with the Naval Postgraduate School in Monterey, Calif. Prior to joining RAND, Chalk served as an assistant professor of politics at the University of Queensland, Brisbane, and a postdoctoral fellow at the Strategic and Defence Studies Centre of the Australian National University, Canberra. In addition to his academic posts, he has acted as a research consultant in the United Kingdom, Canada, and Australia and has experience working with the UK Armed Forces. Chalk has a Ph.D. in political studies from the University of British Columbia, Canada, and a joint masters in international relations and political science from the University of St. Andrews, Scotland.

William Rosenau is a political scientist at RAND's Washington Office and an adjunct professor in the Security Studies Program, Georgetown University. From 2001 to 2002, he served as a policy advisor in the U.S. State Department's counterterrorism office. Rosenau holds a Ph.D. in war studies (King's College, University of London) and an M.A. in history (Magdalene College, Cambridge University).